Frank Houser was immediately a suspect when his girlfriend disappeared, but investigators needed to make a forensic link. They searched Houser's home and could find no signs of a struggle or any clear evidence of blood. They did, however, seize sections of the carpet and pillows that showed unclear stains. Blood was extracted from these items, but who the blood came from was yet to be determined. When the body of the victim was finally recovered, it was so badly decomposed that DNA testing could not be performed. To determine if the carpet and pillow blood matched the victim, investigators tested her parents and obtained a match. This was proof that the victim had been in Houser's apartment and had spilled blood there.

Books published by The Ballantine Publishing Group are available at quantity discounts on bulk purchases for premium, educational, fund-raising, and special sales use. For details, please call 1-800-733-3000.

BLOOD TRAIL

True Crime Mysteries Solved by DNA Detectives

Judge Gerald Sheindlin with Catherine Whitney

BALLANTINE BOOKS • NEW YORK

Copyright © 1996 by Gerald Sheindlin and Catherine Whitney

All rights reserved under International and Pan-American Copyright Conventions. Published in the United States by Ballantine Books, a division of Random House, Inc., New York, and simultaneously in Canada by Random House of Canada Limited, Toronto.

http://www.randomhouse.com

Library of Congress Catalog Card Number: 96-96779

ISBN 0-345-40280-4

Manufactured in the United States of America

First Edition: December 1996

10 9 8 7 6 5 4 3 2 1

To Judy

and to my children—
Greg, Jonathan, Adam,
Jamie, and Nicole

Contents

Contents

Acknowledgments

When I tell people I have written a book, those who know me immediately guess the subject is DNA. What few realize, however, is how daunting a task it is to translate the complexities of science into the flesh-and-blood world we inhabit. For that task, I was fortunate to have much support from people who believed in me and in the dramatic nature of this story.

My collaborator, Catherine Whitney, was immediately fascinated by the gritty reality of the subject. Her enthusiasm and skill helped establish the right tone and kept the narrative as riveting in the telling as it was in real life.

My agent, Jane Dystel, was smart enough to see the potential from the start. She is, indeed, a talented and supportive agent.

Cathy Repetti, my editor at Ballantine, wasn't afraid to plunge into the complicated science of DNA testing. She recognized its great potential as a crime story of modern times. I am thankful for her belief in the project.

Many colleagues have shared my passion for DNA detection, and are dedicated to its proper use in the courtroom. I acknowledge their fine work in the field and their passion for justice, among them: George Clark, Rockne

Harmon, Dr. Eric Lander, Peter Neufeld, Barry Scheck, Peter Coddington, and Risa Sugarman.

A special thanks to my son, Greg, for his legal skills and intelligent suggestions.

Most of all, I am grateful to my wife, Judy, for her patience, humor, and sharp insights. I couldn't have done this without her.

PROLOGUE

Blood Trail . . .

This is the story of the struggle to establish the credibility of this powerful new weapon in the fight against crime.

—HENRY C. LEE, PH.D.
Director, Connecticut State Forensic Laboratory

The Bronx Criminal Courthouse; October 3, 1995

Shortly before 1:00 P.M., I called a lunch recess in my courtroom, where I was hearing a murder case involving a young African American man. We had completed the hearings and were preparing to begin jury selection.

I stepped down from the bench and went into my robing room, a sterile place but for the stunning city view visible through its majestic windows. Several of my personnel were gathered around a small television set. My law secretary, Julia, a smart, charming woman with a winning smile and a sharp sense of humor, shot me a knowing look.

"Any minute now," she said, biting her lower lip in anticipation.

The verdict in the trial of O.J. Simpson was scheduled to be announced at 1:00 P.M., eastern time. I removed my robe, hung it in the closet, and joined the group, not saying anything, but watching intently.

Like most people, I had followed the Simpson case as closely as my schedule allowed, but unlike most, I felt a special interest in the outcome. Although my position as a judge precluded me from discussing my belief in the accused's guilt or innocence, my primary interest was in the use of forensic DNA during the trial. I believed this aspect of the case would have the greatest impact on the future of criminal justice in this country and the world.

It's easy, in such a high-profile case—and this was said a thousand times over—to be distracted by the sideshow, to find important and complex issues reduced to sound bites on the evening news. I tried to look beyond all that to the heart of the case, and I hoped the jury could do the same.

For several years, ever since I was placed in the position to rule on what would be a groundbreaking DNA case in New York (*People v. Castro*), I had been studying this new science, and had now become something of an expert. I often wrote and lectured on the subject, and in January, I would begin teaching a course at Pace University School of Law entitled Criminal Justice: Forensic DNA. It would be the first course of its kind in New York. Finally, the law was catching up with science.

My interest in DNA was passionate and, I felt, profoundly relevant. If the public's collective eyes tended to glaze over during the moments in the trial when scientific complexities were detailed, DNA was nevertheless as compelling as evidence could get. As a judge, I recognized its value, yet I was fearful that it would be too easily disregarded by juries who would be unable to grasp its significance. Jurors are, after all, ordinary citizens and not biologists. They are usually drawn to the type of evidence that is easiest to understand in everyday life, as well as the kind of proof they are familiar with from movies and TV shows. Show them a fingerprint and their eyes will light up. Give them a hair or a thread of cloth or an eyewitness and they'll listen attentively. But DNA—well, that's the technical stuff.

In many respects, the O.J. Simpson case was a classic test of the ability of a lay jury to understand and appreciate the power of DNA evidence. There were no witnesses to the brutal slaying of Nicole Brown Simpson and Ronald Goldman. No murder weapon was ever found. No direct evidence linked O.J. Simpson to the crime—except a small trail of blood, snaking from the murder site to Simpson's bedroom a few miles away.

The process of presenting DNA evidence, the strongest card in the prosecution's deck, was slow and agonizingly complex—it has been compared with some justification to a course in advanced biology. The language and concepts were brain twisters. Scientists talked about "bands" and "strands" and "membranes" and "lanes" and "polymorphic probes" and "restriction fragment length polymorphisms"—while the jury and public struggled to understand. The consensus was that DNA was the most boring aspect of the trial. Yet it was also the most important.

While most people have a hard time following the intricate details of DNA detection, they do understand that the potential impact of this new science in everyday life is nothing short of revolutionary—from the way we prevent and manage disease, to the way we establish paternity, to the way we solve crimes. But the field itself seems too complex and abstract for the majority of us.

We are a long way from perfecting this science. And so, as I sat perched on the edge of a desk and stared at the TV on October 3, I wasn't at all sure of the result. Would the Simpson jury embrace the power of DNA evidence? Would it discount it? As the jurors filed into the courtroom, their faces were blank and unreadable. The court clerk was the only person alive, apart from the jurors themselves, who knew what was contained on that single sheet of paper.

While I waited for the verdict, my thoughts traveled, as they had so many times over the last months, to what the trial might mean for forensic DNA. I hated to admit it, but I felt that the Simpson verdict could make or break this new science for a long time to come. And I was worried because DNA is undoubtedly a mind-bending subject for a jury of twelve ordinary citizens. If only there were a way to really help them see with the shining clarity of a scientist in a lab. Forensic DNA may seem stultifying and obscure, but in reality it is utterly human. There are few subjects more gripping than the drama of blood spilled in violence. That is the true nature of forensic DNA. It is, in essence, a detective's tool. Through DNA, killers, rapists, stalkers, assaulters, and terrorists are brought to justice with the deadly clue found in a drop of blood, a semen stain, the root of a hair, a smear of saliva—a genetic blueprint. Forensic DNA has become a new hero in the pursuit of justice, albeit a hero not yet accorded his due acclaim. I believe it is something of great scientific beauty, yet, like all things human, it has its flaws. This is its story.

CHAPTER 1

Murder in the Bronx

There is a capacity of vice to make your blood creep.

—Ralph Waldo Emerson

The Bronx; February 5, 1987

It was rush hour in the Bronx, the normally congested traffic made worse by the mountains of dirty frozen snow and double-parked cars blocking the narrow streets. Police officers Tony Cruz and Emil Deliberto inched along Jerome Avenue, the wail of their siren having little effect in the heavy traffic. God help you if you had an emergency at 5:45 P.M. on a winter afternoon in this neighborhood, with its glut of a million souls and their various vehicles. If the congestion was maddening enough in itself, gaping potholes and raised slabs of broken, slippery concrete slowed traffic even more.

"Damn!" Deliberto cursed, edging into the right-hand lane that would take him up the Major Deegan Expressway toward Van Cortland Park. It had been ten minutes since the radio crackled, "Burglary in progress, 3415 Knox Place." Time was of the essence, but it was slow going on the Deegan, thanks to the ever present construction that effectively crippled two lanes.

At long last, the officers, siren blaring, sped off the Deegan and along the park. As they turned onto Knox Place with its shabby line of ancient brick apartment buildings, they spotted a tall, young Hispanic man, dressed in rumpled work clothes, frantically waving them to a stop. He identified himself as Jeff Otero.

"Something's wrong!" he cried, leading them at a run up five flights of narrow stairs. The door to apartment 5-C was slightly ajar, and Otero breathlessly told them he hadn't yet been inside. Cruz and Deliberto pulled their guns, pushed open the door, and cautiously entered.

The first thing they saw was a small pool of blood on the floor, surrounded by the eerie stamp of red footprints, and a deep, bloodstained gash in the wall near the door. Motioning Jeff to stand back, the officers stepped carefully into the living room, where they immediately encountered a nauseating scene. Behind them, Jeff let out a howl. On the floor, faceup, her swollen belly protruding and ribboned with knife wounds, lay Jeff's twenty-three-year-old pregnant common-law wife, Vilma.

Cruz and Deliberto were experienced police officers who had seen their fair share of bloody crime scenes. But they never quite got used to it. They were family men, and every crime scene caused their thoughts to race home to their own wives and children. Violence of this magnitude never seems quite real. The very idea that one human being can inflict such harm on another often seems impossible to comprehend.

Vilma Ponce's body lay twisted in an unnatural position, her head resting awkwardly on a sofa cushion that had been pushed to the floor during a struggle. One arm was bent sharply behind her head, the elbow jutting to the side. She was naked from the waist down, her flesh a gruesome crisscross of deep stab wounds. Blood streamed down her bare legs and formed pools under her white socks and sneakers. One of her eyes was half-open. Her mouth formed a silent *O*. The detectives were repulsed to see the remains of her late-term fetus oozing from the cuts in her exposed womb onto the floor.

"I'll check the apartment," Cruz said quietly, moving back down the hall. Deliberto knelt to touch Vilma's body, a hopeless gesture, while Jeff hovered sobbing behind him. "Oh, my God! My baby, my baby. Where's my baby?" he kept saying. Deliberto thought he was talking about the dead fetus.

"I found another one," Officer Cruz called grimly from the other room, and Jeff wailed in anguish and dropped to the floor, cradling his head in his hands. Deliberto hurried down the hallway into the small bathroom and found the slashed body of a two-year-old girl lying on the tile floor in a thick pool of blood. The child's right cheek rested softly against a pile of laundry. Stab wounds formed a wild pattern on her blood-soaked T-shirt and shorts. Her feet in their little yellow sandals were curled inward toward her body in a sleeplike position. Her eyes were half-open, and the curls of her soft brown hair framed her pretty face.

"The first thing I noticed was her face," Cruz would say later. "Peaceful, angelic, her eyes lifted to heaven. Her body was in ribbons, but her face . . ."

Acting quickly now, the two officers secured the scene and called homicide and the medical examiner's office.

A half an hour later, homicide detective Edward Blake arrived at the apartment. Blake was a veteran of the homicide unit, a burly, no-nonsense pro who had seen thousands of deaths in his thirty-year career on the force. He knew all of the ins and outs of the gritty Bronx streets, where poverty and disappointment were part of the landscape. He loved his job, but it was a bittersweet love, for whenever he was called out it was to face a horror like this one.

As Cruz filled him in on the events, Blake wandered slowly through the apartment, running his expert eyes over the scene and all its details. The apartment was old, but well maintained. Numerous photos of a happy family lined the shelves. Mother and child smiled from the pictures. They would never smile again.

The kitchen was spotless, no dishes in the sink. Bloody footprints stood out on the black-and-white floor. Blood was smeared on the sink as though the killer had attempted to wash himself. The faucet was still dripping, turning the deep red of the blood a sickening pink. There was every sign that this was a crime of fury and desperation. Blake concentrated on trying to view the scene through the eyes of the killer. What was the source of his rage? What was the catalyst for his cruelty? Was this the work of a stranger? Was it, heaven forbid, the work of a loved one? There were no ready answers.

Finally, Blake turned his attention to twenty-three-year-old Jeff, huddled in the living room, crying.

"So, what's his story?" Blake asked Deliberto.

"He came home from work, saw something was

wrong, and called us from downstairs. He says he didn't go into the apartment until we got here," Deliberto said.

"Do you know anything about what happened here?" Blake asked Jeff. The young man stared up at him through bleary eyes. His face was a stunned mask of shock and grief.

"I saw him," Jeff choked. "I saw the man who did this."

"Let's take it one step at a time," Blake said, pulling up a chair beside Jeff. In the initial moments of an investigation it is important to stay calm and focused, even when surrounded by such a gruesome scene. The first description of events often turns out to be the most critical. Blake was practiced in the art of questioning people in the initial stages of an investigation, when their guard was down and their composure shaken. He focused intently on Jeff's ravaged face.

Jeff described how he had arrived home at 5:30 in the afternoon from his job as a maintenance worker. When he tried to get into the apartment, the chain lock was on from the inside.

"I go downstairs and call Vilma's mother from the street," he said. "I'm saying, where's Vilma, but she didn't know. I thought maybe she was asleep upstairs, so I go to the alley in back and whistle up to her to wake her up."

Jeff told Blake that while he was in the alley, he saw a man wearing a green hat hurrying out of the basement exit of the building. In the brief seconds that the two men locked eyes, Jeff was stunned to see that the man's face was specked with blood, and his eyes appeared swollen and "chinky"—meaning they had an Asian cast.

As Jeff continued his description, Blake took notes and listened skeptically. Jeff remembered so much about a man of whom he'd caught only a brief glimpse. Was the man real or was he a convenient phantom?

"What did you do then?" he asked.

"I was nervous. I went back upstairs and now the chain was off and the door was open a little. I knew something bad happened."

"Did you go in?"

"No, no," he said. "I looked in and saw the candle. We keep this candle lit every evening, y'know, in a bowl of water by the door. Like a good-luck thing . . . And it was tipped over and spilled, and I knew, oh man, something bad was happening. So I go downstairs and call the police."

Blake looked at Jeff thoughtfully. "Why didn't you go in, if you thought something was wrong?"

Jeff sucked in a deep, shaking breath. "I was scared. I don't know. . . ." He collapsed in a fresh fit of sobbing.

There was something fishy about the story, yet at the same time it was oddly compelling. Blake was suspicious of Jeff, since most murders are committed by people known to the victim—husbands, boyfriends—but he nevertheless listened closely to Jeff's description of the strange man who had emerged from Vilma's basement moments after her death. He waited a couple of minutes for Jeff to regain his composure, then asked, "Do you remember what the guy was wearing?"

"A green hat—it looked bloody. He was wearing jeans,

a beige shirt and jacket. And white Adidas. I remember the Adidas because they have this certain blue stripe on them."

"Okay—anything else?"

Jeff rubbed his eyes, thinking. "There was blood on his wrist," he said suddenly, remembering. "He had a watch—one of those cheap kind with a black plastic band. I saw blood on it."

"Did you speak to him?"

"No . . . no." Jeff shook his head. "But it was weird. As he passed me, we looked right at each other and he smiled. It was the strangest grin. I won't ever forget that."

Edward Blake continued to question Jeff about his movements, focusing on the details that seemed peculiar. The timing seemed to be off. Jeff said the chain lock was on when he got home. But only moments later when he returned from calling Vilma's mother, the chain was off and the door was ajar. It was also ajar when the police arrived. What could have occurred to explain those facts? When he examined the door, Blake noticed that there was no evidence of a forced entry.

A detective of Blake's experience usually had an instinct for when someone was telling the truth. Jeff seemed honestly devastated—but that didn't mean he wasn't the killer. Something in his demeanor, however, didn't jibe with the kind of person who would be the perpetrator of such a horrible scene. Furthermore, as Blake studied Jeff's appearance, he couldn't fail to notice that there were no signs that he had been engaged in any kind of struggle. Whoever had done this would be bloody,

disheveled, and perhaps scratched or cut, and Jeff
was not.

"Can you show me the alleyway where you saw this
guy?" Jeff nodded and led Blake down the long staircase
to the rear of the building. He pointed out the back door,
which stood open, and the walkway that led to the front
of the building. "This is the way he went." He repeated
his description of the mysterious man several times, and
Blake kept asking questions and probing, working over
every detail for a glimmer of insight or an important clue.
In his mind, Jeff was still a suspect. But it was too early
to make a judgment. His first priority was to find the
mystery man, if he really existed.

Vilma Ponce's family had absolutely no use for Jeff
Otero. For years they had begged Vilma to leave this
abusive man. He had a history of physical violence
against Vilma, and had once broken her jaw, an incident
that had landed him in family court.

In the mid-1980s, domestic violence was still poorly
understood and insufficiently reported—especially in
rough neighborhoods like the one Jeff and Vilma inhab-
ited. Even today, the pathology is misunderstood. People
wonder, why does a woman stay with a man who abuses
her? Why does she have children with such a man?

The answer is complicated in a tangle of issues—
socioeconomic status, gender roles, self-esteem. We
know that domestic violence occurs across ethnic, racial,
and class lines. Some experts consider it the leading
health problem of women and children in our society.
Jeff and Vilma's turbulent relationship was like so many

others. When the stress of poverty and life's pressures became too much, when the alcohol flowed freely, arguments turned to violence. Jeff's temper erupted, and he used his fists where reason and hope failed him.

Vilma's family could do little to protect her against Jeff's violence, but they waged an ongoing campaign to convince her to leave him. "Take Natasha and come back home," Vilma's mother begged her. But Vilma always reassured her family that things were working out. Indeed, prior to her latest pregnancy, following the family-court episode, she and Jeff had sought counseling.

"We're okay," Vilma told her mother. "Jeff's working. We're happy."

By all visible signs, this was true. Vilma's face showed optimism and youthful hope. She glowed in anticipation of the birth of her second child. Natasha was a well-cared-for and delightful child. Their family life took on a mellow domesticity that often escapes families in poverty-ridden urban areas. But then everything came to a brutal, bitter stop.

When detectives went to the Ponce apartment to inform Vilma's relatives of the murder, her mother let out a piercing scream, followed by a stream of Spanish fury whose focus was Jeff. She, along with everyone else in the family, was immediately convinced that Jeff the abuser was the murderer. This was simple logic to them. They were angry, adamant, and vocal. They urged the police to arrest him.

When he learned that Jeff had abused Vilma, even once sending her to the hospital emergency room, Blake looked at him with new interest. Although domestic abuse doesn't often lead to murder, statistics show that when an abused woman *is* murdered, the abuser is usually the killer. The nature of this particular crime also pointed to passion and rage—the number of knife wounds, the fury of the attack, the deliberate slashing of Vilma's pregnant belly. It didn't look like the work of a stranger.

Blake was disturbed, however, by the callousness of the child's slaying. Although he had seen cases where a husband or boyfriend slaughtered an entire family, Jeff's intense grief didn't necessarily fit the profile of a domestic-rage killing. It was a piece of the puzzle the detective would have to solve.

It didn't look good for Jeff, but Blake was careful not to jump to conclusions before he had more evidence. There was always the chance that Jeff was telling the truth. In spite of a growing public cynicism about the integrity of law-enforcement officers, veterans like Blake are dedicated to finding the right perpetrator. They aren't interested in railroading a suspect just to make an arrest and leaving the real killer free to kill again. And although Jeff was certainly a suspect, Blake still didn't have enough evidence to make an arrest, despite the urging of Vilma's family. Indeed, apart from Jeff's history of abuse and his presence at the scene, Blake had no evidence against the young man whatsoever.

The next day, Blake returned to the Knox Place building, where he saw the handyman mopping the lobby floor. The man was short, dark, and nervous looking. Blake noticed that his eyes were somewhat puffy; strangely, they had a slight Asian cast—just as Jeff had described. The man looked alarmed when Blake identified himself.

"Can I ask you a few questions?" he asked.

The man shrugged and put down his mop. "Yeah, let's go to my uncle's apartment. He's the super." He led Blake down the hall to a small apartment in the back.

The man said his name was Joseph Castro and he worked for his uncle doing jobs around the buildings in the area.

"Did you notice anything unusual yesterday?" Blake asked. "You know, there was a murder here."

"No, man," Castro said. "I wasn't at this building yesterday."

Blake stared at Castro's left hand. "I see you have a cut on your hand. How'd that happen?"

"I sliced it on the pail I use," Castro said, quickly burying the offending hand in his lap.

"So, you saw nothing?" Blake asked again.

"No, nothing."

Blake stood. "Do you mind if I take your picture?"

Castro shook his head, and tried not to look startled by the request. Blake snapped a picture and turned to leave. "You'll let me know if you think of anything that might help?"

"Oh, sure," Castro said. He seemed relieved. Blake wondered about this guy. He'd have to check him out. And he wanted to show the picture to Jeff—see if it rang any bells.

Later that day, Blake paid Jeff a visit at his uncle's house, where he'd been staying since the murder. He had with him a photo array containing six head shots. Blake had selected five other photos from a drawer at the precinct. They were all male Hispanics, about the same age as Castro. One of the photos was of Castro. Blake wanted to see if Jeff could pick Castro out as being the man he saw in the alley.

Jeff studied the photo array carefully, but failed to identify anyone. "I'd know him if I saw him," he insisted. "But I don't recognize anyone here."

Blake was disappointed. He'd thought he was close, but Jeff's failure to identify Castro stopped him in his tracks. He was also growing increasingly suspicious of Jeff. His suspicion that the description of the strange man in the alley was an invention was growing stronger. Surely, if Jeff's memory was so vivid, he should have been able to identify Castro. It didn't add up.

Jeff knew he was a suspect in the murders. Vilma's family would make sure of that, he thought bitterly. He knew her family despised him and would love nothing more than to see him locked up forever. But he kept insisting, "I didn't do it!" How could anyone think he was capable of such brutality? Sure, he and Vilma had their problems, but the worst was behind them. Things were good now. He was working. They were planning for their new baby. He adored Natasha. There was no way he was capable of this.

Two days after the murder, Jeff returned to Vilma's apartment to get his belongings, accompanied by his aunt and uncle and Detective Blake. It made him physically ill to be in the place, with its lingering bitter scent of death, the stained areas that indicated where his family had been slaughtered, and the white fingerprint dust that coated every surface. It no longer felt like home. He hurriedly threw some clothes in a bag and left the apartment as quickly as he could, parting with Blake on the street.

As his uncle pulled the car away from the curb, Jeff suddenly caught a flash of motion and turned his head sharply. He was shocked to see the man he had seen the day of the murders coming out of the basement. He was with a little girl and was carrying a laundry bag. Jeff noticed immediately that he had cut off his hair.

As the man entered a building next door, Jeff grabbed his uncle's arm and cried, "That's him!" He leaped from the car and raced into the building, not considering the consequences.

"What's your name?" he asked a startled Joseph Castro.

"Joe," the man replied uneasily.

"Smile for me," Jeff demanded, and caught off guard, Castro obliged.

"Thanks," Jeff said softly, then turned and walked out of the building. He broke into a run as he approached the car.

"Drive to the police station!" he ordered his uncle.

He raced into the precinct and excitedly told Blake, "I just saw the man who murdered my family!"

Jeff was outraged and out of control. "He was like a mad man," Blake would say later.

"Let me see the pictures again!" Jeff cried urgently, and bemused, Blake pulled the photo array out of his desk drawer.

Jeff now emphatically pointed out Castro's picture from the same array that he had seen the day before.

"It's him," he said, his voice trembling with emotion. "It's him."

"You're sure?" Blake asked.

"Yes, yes. I saw him. It's him."

Blake wondered how Jeff could be so sure when only one day earlier he hadn't recognized the man at all. And there was another thing. "The man in the picture—his hair is much shorter than the guy you described to us."

"He probably cut it." Jeff shrugged. "It's him." In a breathless rush of words, he described seeing Castro and his absolute certainty that he was the killer.

"It was his smile," he told Blake. "I'll never forget that smile."

Blake was persuaded. He hopped in a car and returned to the building. In the super's apartment, he found Castro relaxing with a beer. Castro clearly wasn't happy to see him.

"Want a beer?" he asked, frowning and squinting his narrow eyes at Blake.

Blake shook his head no. "I want you to come to the station and answer some questions."

Castro took a drink of beer. Blake noticed that his hand was shaking. "Am I under arrest?"

"No," Blake assured him. "No handcuffs. Just talk."

The two men drove in silence to the station, where Blake settled Castro into a small conference room. "Just a few questions," he said casually, opening his notebook.

Castro stared straight ahead. His face showed little emotion.

"You say you weren't anywhere near the building on the day of the murder. . . ." Blake began.

"No, I was working at another place," Castro answered.

"Okay, can you give me that address?"

"Uh . . . I can't remember."

Blake stared at the man for a long silent moment. Did he do it? Was this man a vicious killer? There was something in his eyes—and a man capable of mutilating a pregnant woman and her little daughter *would* have something in his eyes. You could bet on it.

"Tell me about your hand," he said finally.

"I told you," Castro said. "I cut it on a pail."

"Okay, we'll get the pail and check it out."

Then Blake slowly dropped the bombshell. "We have a witness who puts you at the building at the time of the murder."

Castro jumped. "Man, I wasn't there. I told you."

"You think this person is mistaken?"

Castro nodded mutely.

"The witness does say your hair was longer. Did you get it cut recently?"

"Yeah, my mother—" Castro stopped abruptly and bit his lip. Blake smiled serenely. "Your mother gave you a haircut? Fine, I'll talk to her." He stood up. "Just stay put." Blake walked outside the office and told the uniformed officer to keep Castro there until he informed him otherwise. Then he got into his car and drove to a Bronx street several blocks from the murder site and knocked on the door of a small brick row house. Castro's mother was thin and looked old beyond her years. Blake guessed that she'd seen more than one cop at her door.

"Sorry to bother you, ma'am," the detective said

politely. "We're investigating a homicide, and we'd like to see the clippers you used to cut your son's hair recently."

The old woman was baffled. "What's that got to do with a murder?"

"Just procedure," Blake said smoothly. He waited while she got the clippers.

"Can I borrow these, ma'am? I'll make sure they get back to you."

"Yes . . . is Joe a suspect?"

Blake shrugged. "We're just checking every lead. Have a nice day." Then he called the precinct and told the sergeant that Castro could leave.

Edward Blake pondered the facts as he knew them. In spite of Vilma's family's strong belief that Jeff was the murderer, he had to acknowledge that the young man was a hard worker with no prior record. The investigators had thoroughly checked his alibi and found that he'd been at work until 5:00 P.M. on the day of the murders. Blake was beginning to believe that Jeff wouldn't have had enough time to commit the murders. But his identification of Castro was shaky. And he did have a history of violence against Vilma.

Still, there was the strange man, Joseph Castro. He'd had the opportunity. He'd been in the apartment a couple of weeks earlier, "fixing" the lock. And Blake couldn't discount his basic hunch about the guy—his nervousness, his lies. It could mean something—or nothing at all. What was the answer? The pieces gathered by Blake seemed to fit not one, but two puzzles. But looking at the crime-scene photos of the tortured bodies, he knew one thing: whichever man fit the final puzzle, he was a monster.

He thought of the assistant district attorney, a young woman with fire in her belly. Risa will want this guy, he mused grimly. When she sees these bloody pictures, she'll be fighting for an arrest. He slid the pictures into a folder and headed for the district attorney's office.

CHAPTER 2

"I Want Him!"

Did I have enough evidence? I knew I couldn't let
this guy stay on the street.
                                    —RISA SUGARMAN
                                    Assistant District Attorney

Assistant District Attorney Risa Sugarman sat in her
office at the Bronx Criminal Court building, overlooking
Yankee Stadium, and cleared a space amid the jumble of
files on her cluttered desk. It had already been a long day,
and Risa was tired. What little makeup she'd worn that
morning had long since faded during the intense activity
of a typical workday. She rubbed her eyes beneath her
large-framed glasses and studied the photos of Vilma
Ponce and her daughter, Natasha. Blake was right: Risa
wanted the man who did this. In her career, the assistant
DA had seen many such photos, but she had never grown
inured to their horror. If anything, the brutality of the
scene only strengthened her conviction about the right-
ness of her choice to work as a lawyer.

You might say Risa was a career prosecutor. She'd
joined the DA's office right out of law school and never
looked back. She was tough and smart, an excellent
investigator, and a superb trial lawyer. Around the courthouse, everyone agreed that if Risa got her hooks in you,
you were as good as convicted. She was relentless, a

single woman whose job was her life. After this matter was concluded, Risa would marry one of the homicide detectives who worked on the case, and they would have a son. But for now, her absolute focus was bringing a sadistic killer to justice.

As she did in every murder case, Risa regarded herself as the lone voice speaking for the dead victims who could no longer speak for themselves. The heart of justice, she believed, was never to let the murdered die silently and anonymously. A human life was worth something. It was worth everything.

Risa brushed feathery blond curls from her face and kicked off her high heels. As the sun set in silvery streaks on the stadium behind her, she pored over the files. When the chief of the DA's homicide bureau had given her the file, he seemed hesitant. "I don't think we have enough evidence on this guy to warrant an arrest," he told her. Now, as she focused closely on the files, she was hoping to prove him wrong.

Vilma had been stabbed sixty-seven times. Her naked lower body indicated that this was a rape that had been interrupted—possibly by Jeff's attempt to enter the apartment.

Little Natasha's sweet face haunted Risa. The child had twenty-eight stab wounds, deep and fatal, to her front and back. Risa suspected that the terrified youngster had run frantically from the killer and the killer had chased her through the apartment, stabbing feverishly, before he cornered her in the bathroom. The horror the child must have felt was unimaginable, yet her stilled face was clear and unmarked by blood or terror.

Risa turned her attention to the forensic evidence from the police and the coroner's office and the description of Castro. For the past month, she had been working on another homicide that had occurred a couple of blocks away from Vilma's apartment; it bore similarities to this one. She noted that Castro also worked in that building as a handyman. In this case as well, the victim had been brutally slashed and raped, and Castro had been observed trying to enter the woman's apartment a day before the murder. The similarity was painfully obvious. But there was no hard evidence.

Investigative work is a grueling process of building a pattern of evidence from the tiniest of scraps. A hair, a fiber, a speck of blood. In Risa's opinion, there were details in the forensic evidence in the murder of Vilma and Natasha that seemed to point to Castro—most notably, the green fibers that had been collected. A microscopic analysis of the clippers Castro's mother had given to Blake revealed green threads that matched the ones the police had removed from Natasha's clothing. This also supported Jeff's assertion that Castro was wearing a green hat, although no hat had been recovered.

There was also the matter of Castro's presence in the building. He had told investigators he wasn't there that day, and he was sticking to his story. But Risa was pretty sure he was lying. She had statements from several tenants other than Jeff who had spotted him at the building.

When Detective Blake asked him about the cut on his hand, Castro said he'd cut it on a metal pail. But although the police checked all the pails used, they never found a pail that matched the cut or that yielded any traces of blood.

They also had the statement of a girlfriend of Vilma's. She had told the detectives about an unpleasant incident that occurred a couple of weeks before the murder. She and Vilma were walking down the street when they passed the handyman who worked in Vilma's building. "Vilma said she was afraid of that guy. She didn't like the way he looked at her." The comment, of course, had no evidentiary meaning. You can't arrest someone because they look at you funny. But Risa was interested in it nonetheless, being, as it was, another mention of Joseph Castro's name.

Before she left for the night, Risa walked back to the video office and pushed the crime-scene tape into a VCR. Sitting alone in front of the TV screen, she watched the slow, silent film recording of the scene of Vilma and Natasha's horrible deaths. The camera traveled through the apartment, lingering on the neat, polished surfaces, the family photos that showed a beautiful young Vilma, the glowing face of a woman with promise, the happy smiles of family and friends, the baby pictures of Natasha. Then, abruptly, it shifted to Vilma's crumpled half-naked body, resting against the sofa cushion that had been roughly pushed to the floor. She was barely recognizable as the pretty woman in the pictures. In death, after all the brutality, Vilma had been made to look ugly. Her face was unreadable. Risa could only imagine the young mother's final thoughts. Her body was a sea of wounds, and the camera paused at her belly, detailing incision after incision.

When the camera finally moved away from Vilma, it traveled down a narrow hallway, following bloody shoeprints to a small bathroom where Natasha lay, curled in a fetal position on the floor. Her back and legs were soaked with blood, but her sweet face was untouched and quiet in repose. Were it not for the blood, you might have thought she was sleeping.

At last, mercifully, the camera moved away, back down the hallway to the kitchen. It lingered on the sink with its telltale pool of bloodstained water.

Risa shut off the VCR and removed the cassette, returning it to the drawer. She felt tired and tearful. Maybe people thought you became hardened to these scenes, and God knows, she was a tough professional. But each time she saw one, the tragedy and waste and horror struck her anew—as if it were the first time she had ever viewed a bloody scene. She thought of all the people who were, at the very moment of the murder, arriving home from work, cooking dinner, laughing and sweeping their children into warm embraces. Their attention would be on the mundane and comforting details of their own lives. They could not know that at that very moment, a young woman who lived in a ghetto in a city that housed millions, would be snuffed out forever. A little girl would not be running to hug her father when he came home from work. A baby would never be born. These were not faceless statistics. They were real. It would be Risa's task to bring them alive for a jury. But first, the killer must be caught.

"I went home that night feeling scared," Risa would later recall. "I was worried that the same person who murdered Vilma and Natasha might also be the one who committed the homicide two blocks away the previous month. If that were true, we were dealing with a serial killer, and in my experience a serial killer's urges came upon him at specific intervals—in a cyclical pattern. If this murderer was on a cycle, another killing could take place in weeks.

"With what I knew about Castro, I couldn't let him stay on the street."

The next day, Risa obtained a search warrant to seize sneakers from Castro's apartment. She had examined the bloody footprints left on the apartment floor and knew they were made by sneakers. Witnesses had said that Castro often wore sneakers, and Jeff had a vivid recollection of Castro's Adidas on the day of the murders. The assistant DA wanted to see if she could get a match with the bloody footprints left at the scene. Police searched his apartment and found one pair of white Adidas sneakers. As it turned out, the shoes matched the bloody footprint. Furthermore, it was determined that Castro's white Adidas had recently been scrubbed clean. This, in itself, seemed odd, since Castro himself told the detectives that he wore the sneakers every day.

Risa instructed that the actual sections of the floor containing the bloody footprints be cut out and preserved as evidence.

Armed with the forensic evidence that supported her opinion, Risa went to her superior and argued passionately for Castro's arrest:

"Let me tell you what I think happened. I think Castro was planning to rape Vilma. We have evidence that Castro changed the locks on her apartment a couple of weeks before the murder. We think he fixed the lock in such a way that the door couldn't be securely locked. On the afternoon of the murder, he let himself into Vilma's apartment and put the chain lock on the door. He forced Vilma to remove her clothes from the waist down, and she complied. But she was extremely frightened because her small daughter was in the apartment. Vilma began to struggle with him, and he grew infuriated. Those stab wounds show anger and hatred. He was out of control."

Risa paused and looked at her notes. "Natasha, poor baby, probably heard or saw the whole thing. It looks like Castro chased her through the apartment and finally caught her in the bathroom. She fought him, too. Both of them fought him. I think the knife slipped because of all the blood and that's how he got the cut on his hand.

"Jeff came home, probably at the point Castro was washing the blood off in the kitchen. Jeff couldn't get in because the chain was on. No sounds were coming from the apartment because his family was no doubt already dead. He went downstairs to the alley, and Castro fled, leaving the door ajar. He encountered Jeff in the alley only moments later. That's why I think he'd already committed the murders by the time Jeff arrived.

"We have reasonable cause to arrest this guy. I want him."

Risa had made her case. An arrest was authorized and Joseph Castro was picked up and brought to the station. There, police photographed the cut on his hand. They also noted that he was wearing the watch with the black plastic strap that Jeff had mentioned. There was a small rust-colored spot on the face of the watch.

Edward Blake confronted him. "It looks like blood."

Castro shrugged, pretending indifference. "If it's blood, it's my blood."

Blake took the watch from Castro's wrist. Later, when the watch was opened, more rust-colored spots could be seen on the inside.

Serology tests proved that the stain was human blood—consistent with Vilma's blood type, not Castro's.

The evidence was falling into place against Castro. But there were several problems that continued to trouble Risa. First and foremost, no one had seen Castro commit the murders, nor was the murder weapon ever found. The green hat, the probable source of the fibers, was missing. Jeff's initial identification was faulty, and his own history of abuse against Vilma weighed heavily on Risa's mind.

If only there was some way to put Castro in the apartment! If the blood on Castro's watch could be identified with greater certainty as Vilma's, the case would come together. Serology tests helped some, but they weren't conclusive, since many people have the same blood type.

Recently, Risa had read about a remarkable case in Florida where DNA evidence had been used to catch a serial rapist. The rapes—at least twenty-three of them— occurred during 1986, and police suspected the same man was responsible for all of them since the pattern was so eerily similar. All of the attacks occurred in the dead of night, inside the women's homes. The rapist seemed to choose his victims carefully, stalking them in advance and learning everything he could about them. To one woman he said, "I've seen what you do with your boy-friend. Now I want you to do the same with me."

The rapist was careful. He covered his victims' heads with a sheet during the rapes, and they could not identify him. Only one victim got a six-second view of his face, and that wasn't enough. He was careful to leave no fingerprints. But he did leave behind one clue: his semen.

One night, plainclothes policemen covering the area of the rapes got lucky. A woman called in to report a prowler. When the police responded, they spotted a blue Ford Grenada speeding away from the area. They followed the car as it careened along the dark streets and finally crashed into a utility pole. The driver was a twenty-four-year-old man named Tommie Lee Andrews.

Forensic DNA testing was virtually unknown at the time, but like Risa, prosecutor Tim Berry had heard about it. He sent a sample of Andrews's blood, along with the semen samples, to Lifecodes, a genetic testing laboratory then located in Valhalla, New York. There was a match. Tommie Lee Andrews was identified as the contributor of the semen. He was convicted and sentenced to over one hundred years in prison.

Risa was impressed with DNA testing. She decided to use this new forensic test to see if she could get a positive identification for the blood on Castro's watch as Vilma's or Natasha's. Risa had a decent case even without the DNA, but she was convinced that this new forensic evidence would make it overwhelming. However, the testing was going to be difficult because there was only a small amount of blood residue on the watch. She decided to take a chance. She requested and received a court order directing that a sample of Castro's blood be taken. This was accomplished and the sample was sent to

Lifecodes. Then Risa retrieved the watch from the medical examiner's office, where it had been stored after the serological tests, and personally delivered it to Lifecodes. As she drove up the New York Thruway, her resolve deepened. She wanted this killer so bad she could taste it. And she was convinced that Joseph Castro was her man.

Before the DNA tests were even completed, Risa presented her case to a grand jury and got an indictment against Castro for the murders of Vilma and Natasha. Several members of the grand jury urged her to indict Castro for the murder of the fetus as well. She refused, reluctantly.

"The death of the fetus was a horrible thing," she reflected later. "But by law, a person is defined as being born and alive. I couldn't take the chance that the case would get bogged down in a fight about whether a fetus is a human being and whether Vilma's fetus was alive and born. I wanted the case to be clear-cut."

When the DNA test results were received, they showed a match between Vilma's DNA and the bloodstains scraped from Castro's watch. That might have sealed the case for the prosecution. Instead, the DNA results opened up a can of worms.

I had been appointed to the criminal court by New York City mayor Edward Koch in 1983. I was designated to be a New York State Supreme Court judge in 1986. When I was assigned to be the supreme court judge in the Castro case, I had only been on the bench for three years.

I was completely committed to the law and my work,

but I think I looked at the world and the criminal-justice system through a unique lens. When a defendant stood before me, especially a young kid, I always thought, "This could have been me." I never stopped thinking about myself as Jerry Sheindlin from the Bronx.

The tough streets of the Bronx were home to me. It's where my parents settled when they emigrated to the United States from Russia in the 1920s. They were poor and extremely authoritarian. My mother was physically strict, as was her mother before her, and this in turn inspired my rebellion. I became a serious discipline problem at home and at school. I actually liked to fight, but unfortunately, I was small and thin, so I usually lost. When I arrived home with my clothes muddy and torn and my usual black eye and bloody nose, my mother would take out the strap or broom handle for yet another round. It didn't work.

I was troubled, but street-smart. My two sisters and I attended the same school, and my teachers were always giving them notes to take home to our parents requesting that they come in to discuss my behavior. I would intercept my sisters and the notes before they reached home, and threaten dire consequences if they delivered them.

Finally, after having sent home many notes without a response, one of my teachers confronted me. "Are your parents coming in?" she asked sternly.

I was quick on my feet—a lawyer in the making. With suddenly tearful eyes, I told her, "They can't visit. They're dead."

She melted. "You poor child!" she cried, believing that deep grief made me misbehave. With the logic of an eleven-year-old, I thought my troubles were finally over. It never occurred to me that word of my parents' "death" would reach my sisters and they would spill the beans. That night, a note from my teacher was finally delivered to my mother, and the memory of that night lingers. The brutality that followed was so severe that my screams caused the neighbors to call the police.

My youth was further plagued by severe asthma. When my family began spending summers at a small house in Shenorock, New York, I couldn't join them because of my condition, which the lush landscape, with its trees and grass, would cause to immediately flare up. Thus I spent many summers at home in the Bronx, working at a grocery store. I also worked at the New Kentucky Riding Stables on Pelham Parkway. My "pay" consisted of one hour of free riding, and this became my passion.

I went to DeWitt Clinton High School, an all-boys school. Youth gangs were rampant in those days, the most intimidating being the Fordham Baldies. Seven of us from our neighborhood decided that we would form a gang. But we were all very short and thin. We decided to call ourselves the Kingsbridge Munchkins. As I think back, the name hardly sounds intimidating. I guess we tried to scare people with the size of our pompadours and the peg in our pants. That we were rarely successful should come as no surprise.

I barely graduated high school with a 68 average, and I suppose had it not been for the Korean War, my course as a young punk would have been set. But I, along with the rest of the Kingsbridge Munchkins, joined the navy right out of high school.

It was my salvation. Or rather, a man named Dr. Henry Bouchard was. He changed my life, and not a day goes by on the bench when I don't think that every kid deserves the chance I got, and that we adults really can make an impact on young lives.

Dr. Bouchard was a young physician from Vermont in charge of the sick bay aboard the U.S.S. *Staten Island*. I was assigned to be his assistant, and he took a liking to me, despite my thick Bronx accent, seeing something in me that I couldn't see myself. Bouchard taught me everything there was to know about the sick bay, the medicines, the signs and symptoms of common ailments, the art and technique of various procedures. I was like a sponge. I couldn't believe this strange and wonderful experience of being needed, of knowing the answers, of being respected and liked.

I still remember the pride that filled me when the ship's newspaper featured me as the Sailor of the Month. I'd never appreciated the regard my shipmates had for me. The article detailed how they found me sympathetic to their troubles and how I always knew the right medicine to use for their problems. I never dreamed they felt that way about me. I was overcome with a warm feeling of belonging.

The memory of that period and the change it wrought in me has shaped many of my decisions when I deal with young offenders. I know how to look past the tough veneer and the crude language. I try to scratch the surface to find out if there is another Jerry Sheindlin underneath. I try to give something back.

It is amazing how the navy experience transformed me. Suddenly I was a new person, armed with fresh self-confidence. I began to apply to various colleges to begin my journey to a fulfilling career. But, like an explosion, the reality of my early years of misbehavior and poor grades disrupted my dreams. My parents advised me to forget about college and get a job.

One day, I sat down with my father. He was not an educated man, but he had native smarts. I had never before talked to him about things that mattered to me. We just didn't do that in my family. But this was urgent. I had been rejected by every college to which I had applied. I looked my father in the eye and told him of my great disappointment and deep depression.

He shrugged. "I always said you'd be a bum," he replied gruffly. But he softened when he saw my eyes fill with tears. I was tough and I rarely cried.

My father's tone changed. "One of the tenants in a building I manage is a college professor," he said. "Let me see if I can do something. He's always bothering me about needing a new refrigerator."

I later learned that the professor received an expensive refrigerator. I received something of far greater value—a letter of admission to Long Island University. I didn't blow my big chance. My college and law-school grades were excellent. And I found I had a passion for the law.

The succeeding years, as I began my practice and started my family, were the best of my life. I still could hardly believe that the old Jerry Sheindlin from the

Bronx was really me. After twenty years as a trial lawyer, I was selected to be a criminal court judge, and I took to it with my typical fervor. If for the most part, the defendants who appeared before me were headed for state prison and probably a lifetime of alienation from society, I relished the occasional payback—the thing that made my job worth doing—discovering a young kid who reminded me of myself. I had the power to give such a kid a hand up into society, and I did so. I often thought that if a judge's only responsibility were to send people to prison, what a miserable job that would be. There had to be more—and I looked for it. Because of my own background, I rarely felt contempt for the young people who appeared before me. I tried to see them as individuals with possibility. Being a judge filled me with tremendous satisfaction, and I thought I was good at my job. I wasn't scared by a tough legal challenge.

Now, as I reviewed the details of the Castro case, I immediately saw that the challenge was massive—far outside my experience. That challenge was called DNA.

CHAPTER 3

A Genetic Fingerprint

I had never before run up against an area of the
law that couldn't be mastered with some effort
and hard work.

—JUDGE SHEINDLIN

Forensic DNA had first gained notoriety in the mid-
1980s when it was used to solve the grisly rape and
murder of two British schoolgirls. Fifteen-year-old
Lynda Mann and fourteen-year-old Dawn Ashforth were
violently raped and murdered on a deserted pathway in
the small village of Norborough, nearly three years apart.
The murders baffled the local police, who were unaccus-
tomed to such terrible crimes in their bucolic community.

After long years of tireless investigation, their search
led them to a convincing suspect—a young man who was
well known locally for his strangeness. When the suspect
admitted to the murders and even described them, the
entire community breathed a sigh of relief.

At the same time, at nearby Leicester University, a
thirty-four-year-old scientist named Alec Jeffreys had
just discovered something truly remarkable. Using newly
developed genetic engineering techniques for looking at
DNA, Jeffreys was able to distinguish variations that
amounted to a genetic fingerprint.

When the Norborough investigators learned of Jeffreys's work, they decided to seal their case by sending samples of the suspect's blood along with semen samples from the two murders.

When the results were in, Jeffreys placed a call to the chief superintendent, and began the conversation with the words, "I have good news and bad news."

The bad news was astonishing: the suspect they were so certain of was absolutely not the contributor of the semen, and therefore not the murderer.

The good news? "You're only looking for one suspect," Jeffreys told him. The samples from both girls showed that one man had committed both rapes.

The police were back to square one and feeling deeply discouraged. If not their prime suspect, who, then, had committed the crimes? It occurred to them that they might make further use of Alec Jeffreys's expertise.

All along, the police had believed that the killer was living among them. Since the population of the area was only a few thousand, perhaps they could begin using a process of elimination, by DNA, that would eventually lead them to a match. That's how it came to pass that in a remarkable and totally unprecedented effort to find the killer, the police made an appeal to the community. All males between the ages of seventeen and thirty-four were asked to voluntarily give a blood sample. In what was termed a "blooding" (later described in Joseph Wambaugh's best-seller *The Blooding*), they set out to collect and test the blood of all men in the area who might have committed the rape-murders. It was an incredibly complex and time-consuming task. Within nine months, investigators had collected more than 4,500 blood samples, representing, they believed, every man in the area. But they had yet to find a match. There were, it seemed, two possibilities: either the murderer did not live in the area, as they had thought, or DNA tests were not really reliable.

But it turned out that there was another possibility. One evening, the manager of a local bakery was talking about the case in a pub with some of her employees when she learned that a man who worked for her, Colin Pitchfork, had persuaded another employee to give blood in his stead.

The bakery manager reported the news to police, who questioned the surrogate donor. He admitted that he had given blood in Pitchfork's place. The following morning, police went to Pitchfork's home. Moments after they arrested him, he confessed. But his confession was anticlimactic because his blood proved a perfect match to the semen found in the two victims.

Now DNA was the hot new star in the forensic community. Although the science was young, it was already being used as a critical weapon in the courtroom. Not only could DNA tests point the finger at the true criminal, they could also definitely exclude a person who was not guilty.

The potential of DNA testing was seductive to the law-enforcement community. Imagine the possibilities! A mere drop of blood to trace a killer. A smear of semen to catch a rapist. It was as revolutionary a discovery as the use of fingerprints; indeed, even more revolutionary. Criminals excelled in masking their fingerprints with gloves or wiping surfaces that they touched. Even when they weren't so careful, partial prints often yielded no firm results. They often didn't adhere properly to certain surfaces—the ridged butt of a gun, for example.

DNA, on the other hand, was present in small samples of blood, semen, tissue, saliva, and other cellular substances. It was like a "super-fingerprint," and thus potentially the most decisive discovery ever to be made in the field of forensic investigation.

As I studied the casework involving DNA, searching for clarity, a particularly gruesome and fascinating story caught my eye. Just recently, a man named Timothy Spencer had been convicted in Arlington, Virginia, of a series of rapes and murders that occurred over a four-year period. Although the murders were committed in two different cities, Arlington and Richmond, nearly one hundred miles apart, the method was so similar that investigators were convinced the same man had performed them. In each case, the killer entered a house at night through an open or broken window and surprised the women in their beds. The women were raped, tortured, and strangled by an elaborately designed noose bound around the neck and hands. Autopsy evidence showed that the killer lingered over the deaths, tightening then loosening the noose again and again before finally killing his victims.

While investigators knew the killer was intelligent and cautious, they had managed to determine little else about him. Surfaces at the scenes were wiped clean, no fingerprints were left; and except for the deathbeds themselves, there was no evidence of a struggle. Nor were there witnesses or other clues to point to the identity of the killer.

Spencer did, however, leave one calling card in every instance: his semen.

I read with fascination about Joe Horgas, a determined detective who, with virtually no evidence but semen, brought Spencer to justice, with the help of Lifecodes, the very laboratory to which the Castro evidence had been sent. Spencer himself made one fatal error; he willingly gave a sample of his blood, failing to understand that the genetic material contained in blood was also contained in semen. It was remarkable to me that a case of such magnitude could be solved beyond a reasonable doubt with genetic testing. Spencer proclaimed his innocence to the end, but science was more persuasive.

Even so, I entered the world of DNA science with trepidation. In order to grasp the impact of DNA in the case, I had to understand it myself—to be able to visualize it in my mind, and that presented perhaps the biggest challenge of my career. I was determined to become knowledgeable enough so I wouldn't be out of control in my courtroom—putty in the hands of lawyers and scientists who understood this stuff. A judge isn't just ornamental, after all. He has a heavy obligation to see that justice is done. How can he achieve that if he doesn't understand the science brought before him?

So I began the grueling process of educating myself. Almost immediately, I ran into a wall. The terminology swam before me. I felt as if I were reading a foreign language. In desperation, I called my son, Jonathan, who was in medical school.

"I need all the information you can give me about DNA," I told him urgently.

I could hear Jonathan yawn on the phone. "Dad, are you aware that it's one o'clock in the morning?"

"Oh, sorry . . ." I hadn't noticed the time. I was possessed with learning about this new field.

My first task was to understand what the hell DNA was. This was awesome due, quite literally, to the sheer magnitude of the subject. I wasn't used to thinking in trillions! But there it was. There are approximately 100 trillion cells in the human body and most of them contain DNA.

DNA (deoxyribonucleic acid) is like a huge manual, contained in almost every cell, that holds all of the instructions necessary to build a living organism. You might say that DNA is the blueprint for building a living organism. Every living thing has DNA—plants, animals, and humans. Humans have human form and elephants have elephant form because of differences in the makeup of their respective DNA. Within humans, as a species, much of the DNA is identical. It is this similarity of DNA that makes all humans look like humans, rather than like dogs or trees. We humans create human offspring by transferring our DNA to our children.

The easiest way to visualize what DNA looks like is to think of a long spiral staircase. The handrails and balustrade of the staircase consist of repeated sequences of phosphate and deoxyribose sugar. The steps of the staircase are composed of pairs of four types of organic bases, which are identified by their initial letter: (A) adenine, (G) guanine, (C) cytosine, and (T) thymine. These pairs are connected by hydrogen bonds, and because of the chemical nature of these bonds, only A and T can bind together, and only G and C can bind together. A cannot bind with G and C cannot bind with T. So the only possible combinations that can form the steps of the staircase are A-T, T-A, C-G, and G-C.

A single DNA molecule consists of about three billion base pairs, wound tightly into the spiral form. Although it is too small to be seen with even the most powerful microscope, if it were stretched out to its full length, it would be about six feet long. If it were reduced to a written representation, the genetic information contained in a single human DNA molecule would fill about 125 Manhattan telephone books. It would be about one million pages—seventy yards thick with genetic information, spelled out using only the four letters of the DNA language—ATGC.

What determines a person's unique DNA? Each normal human has forty-six chromosomes. Twenty-two come from the mother and twenty-two come from the father. In addition, each person has two sex chromosomes; females have X and X, and males have X and Y. Within the chromosomes are about 100,000 paired genes made of DNA.

The sequence of the three billion base pairs along the handrails of the DNA is the key to the information represented by the DNA. Most of the DNA in humans is alike. Regularly formed humans all have two arms, two legs, two eyes, two ears, and so on. Scientists have identified about 10 percent of these base pairs responsible for producing arms, legs, kidneys, brain cells, and so on.

The Structure of DNA

DNA, found in blood, semen, saliva, hair, tissue, bone marrow, teeth, and urine, appears like a long spiral staircase, whose handrails and balustrade are composed of phosphate and deoxyribose sugar. The steps are comprised of pairs of four types of organic bases:

 (A) Adenine

 (G) Guanine

 (C) Cytosine

■ (T) Thymine

SCHULER

Now, within each human there are obvious genetic differences, or alternate forms of genes, known as alleles. All humans have thousands of genes located on each of the forty-six chromosomes. Alternate forms of these genes determine whether you have blue, violet, brown, or black eyes, are tall or short, fat or thin. Alleles are formed by differences in the sequence of base pairs. For example:

Person 1: A T T C
             T A A G

Person 2: A T A C
             T A T G

Each of these sequences is actually quite long—about 10,000 base pairs. Very small variations in the order of these base pairs on the DNA molecule can make a big difference. Sickle-cell anemia, for example, is caused by a single base pair on a single gene on the eleventh chromosome occurring out of order. Say, a G exists where there should be an A. If that lone aberrant base pair were properly placed, the person would not have the disease. Lou Gehrig's disease is caused by a single base pair out of place on the twenty-first chromosome. Amazingly, each chromosome has about one million base pairs.

But within each individual's DNA, in between the genes, there is also material that scientists have been unable to understand. These sequences repeat themselves in a stutter between the genes and seem to make no sense at all. It would be comparable to finding pages

Your DNA Inheritance

Each person's chromosomes are inherited from his father and his mother in a special way to make his DNA utterly unique.

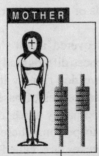

MOTHER

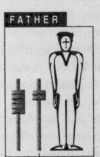

FATHER

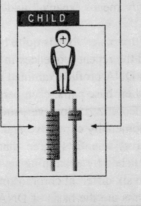

CHILD

SCHALER

of gibberish scattered throughout an instruction manual. Of course, in the grand scheme of things, this apparent gibberish no doubt has—or had—a purpose. Some scientists speculate it's leftover "instructions" from prehistoric times. We are, however, unable to make sense of it now.

So, in the midst of a known DNA sequence that forms a gene, these gibberish repetitions will appear. An example would be if you were reading an instruction manual and suddenly the word "cat" was repeated over and over again, hundreds of thousands of times, between the pages of instructions.

One thing scientists have discovered about this so-called junk DNA is that the sequences differ greatly from person to person. So, although we don't know its purpose, we can use these varying sequences of base pairs to single out individuals. Approximately three million of these sites vary from person to person. These varying repeat sequences between genes are called polymorphisms. *Poly* means "many," and *morphism* means "form."

The issue of forensic DNA is quite basic: how do you accurately read the repeat sequences in genetic material? Obviously, if a DNA profile examined all forty-six chromosomes and their base pairs, each person's DNA could be positively recognized. However, such an undertaking would be phenomenally expensive and time-consuming. As an alternative, scientists agree that individuals can also be distinguished by examining several polymorphic sites on three to six different chromosomes.

Polymorphisms are the basis of DNA identification—the genetic fingerprint, so to speak—using a method

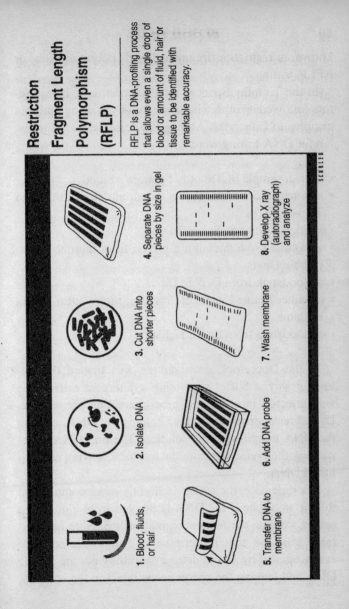

Restriction Fragment Length Polymorphism (RFLP)

RFLP is a DNA-profiling process that allows even a single drop of blood or amount of fluid, hair or tissue to be identified with remarkable accuracy.

1. Blood, fluids, or hair

2. Isolate DNA

3. Cut DNA into shorter pieces

4. Separate DNA pieces by size in gel

5. Transfer DNA to membrane

6. Add DNA probe

7. Wash membrane

8. Develop X ray (autoradiograph) and analyze

SCHELER

known as restriction fragment length polymorphism, or RFLP, testing.

In the Timothy Spencer serial-murder case, investigators followed an otherwise weak trail by sending multiple samples to Lifecodes. Among the items delivered to the lab for DNA testing were:

- a fresh sample of Timothy Spencer's blood
- a semen-stained nightgown from murder victim Susan Tucker
- a bloodstain from Susan Tucker
- a vaginal swab containing semen from murder victim Debbie Davis
- a bloodstain from Debbie Davis
- a semen-stained blanket from murder victim Susan Hellams
- a bloodstain from Susan Hellams

In the laboratory, each sample was treated the following way: a buffer containing a detergent called lysis was injected into the test tube containing the sample. Lysis breaks open the nucleus holding the DNA, causing the DNA to spill into the solution. The non-DNA material was then removed from the test tube, leaving concentrated DNA.

In a rape case, the matter is slightly more complicated than it would be if the DNA is derived from blood. In a semen sample, the female vaginal cells have to be separated from the male's sperm cells. The female cells are easily opened by a mild detergent spilling out the female DNA and leaving the sperm heads intact in the solution.

The concentrated female DNA is then removed. A second solution is used to break open the sperm head that contains the male DNA. In this manner, it is possible to separately test the male and female DNA.

The second step is to "cut" the DNA into shorter pieces so the sequences can be read. This is done with a restriction enzyme, a genetically engineered "scissors" that recognizes particular sequences whenever they appear—for example, sequences that begin AG and end CC. Once these sequences have been cut, they form different lengths of DNA.

Next, a tray of Jell-O-like substance is prepared, with separate lanes. At the top of this gel, the sample material is loaded into slots:

TS: Spencer's blood
US-1: unknown semen stain one
ST: Susan Tucker's blood
US-2: unknown semen stain two
DD: Debbie Davis's blood
US-3: unknown semen stain three
SH: Susan Hellam's blood

The samples are surrounded by what are called marker lanes. In these lanes, DNA of known lengths are placed to serve as a measurement. The markers are comparable to DNA rulers that measure the number of repeat sequences.

A weak electric current is passed through the gel. DNA has a natural negative electrical charge and flows toward the positively charged end of the gel. As the DNA from the individual lanes travels downward, the larger

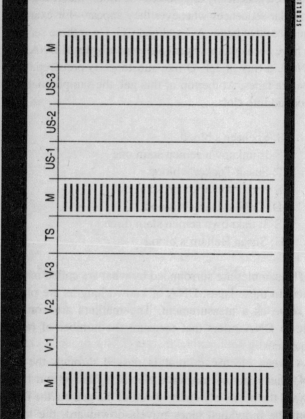

The gel in the Spencer case was composed of markers identifying the three victims and Spencer, with the three unknown semen samples. M stands for the marker lanes: V-1, V-2, and V-3 are blood samples from the three victims (Susan Tucker, Debbie Davis, and Susan Hellams); TS is blood taken from Timothy Spencer; US-1, US-2, and US-3 are the three unknown semen stains.

M   V-1   V-2   V-3   TS   M   US-1   US-2   US-3   M

DNA material (containing the most base pairs) stays toward the top, and the lighter material (containing the fewest base pairs) flows to the bottom.

The next step involves the process of reading the results, but in order to do that, the information contained in the gel has to be transferred to a more solid material. This is done through a process called Southern blot, named for Dr. Edward Southern, a Scottish biochemist who developed the technique.

First, the pairs of DNA in the gel are unzipped into single strands by a chemical that dissolves the bonds holding A to T and G to C. Rather than looking like this:

A C T G
T G A C

. . . they now look like this:

A C T G
    T G A C

These strands are then transferred to a sheet of nylon, fixing each of them into a permanent position on the sheet.

Now the DNA is ready to be identified. This is done with a genetic probe of known sequences of base pairs tagged with radioactive markers. The probe seeks out and bonds with its complement, much like a key that fits only one lock. Or imagine a genetic magnet looking for a needle in a haystack. When it finds the needle, it attaches itself to it and leaves the rest of the hay undisturbed.

After the probe binds to the membrane, excess probe is washed, leaving only the probe that binds to an allele.

Finally, the marked nylon is placed on a piece of X-ray film where the radioactive probes expose the film at their respective locations.

Dark bands resembling supermarket bar codes appear on the X-ray film where the radioactive probes bond with the RFLPs. This produces the print, called an autoradiograph, or autorad.

Lisa Bennett, the technician from Lifecodes, placed the long-awaited call to Detective Horgas.

"Good news," she said simply.

"Yes!" Horgas screamed. The results showed that it was virtually certain that Timothy Spencer had committed all three murders. (He was later convicted and sentenced to death.)

I was particularly interested in samples in the Spencer case that were too degraded for RFLP testing. One of the rape-murders occurred as far back as 1984 and the semen was degraded. What could we do with a sample that was infinitesimal or degraded? Unlike a clinical scientist who can easily procure a substantial amount of uncontaminated material, the forensic scientist must work with what he is given.

Degraded or small samples present a special challenge. RFLP testing is extremely difficult to perform on these. Another method, called polymerase chain reaction (PCR), is used. While PCR is less conclusive than RFLP, it is far more conclusive than a standard ABO blood

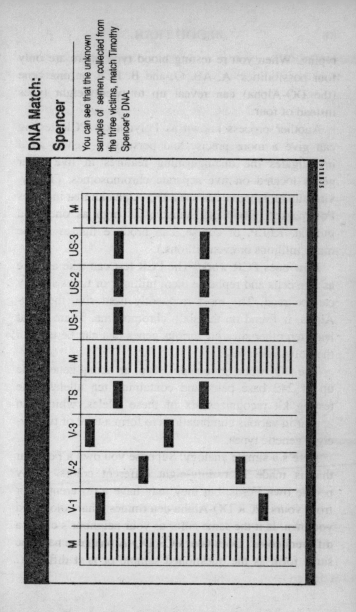

DNA Match: Spencer

You can see that the unknown samples of semen, collected from the three victims, match Timothy Spencer's DNA.

M US-3 US-2 US-1 M TS V-3 V-2 V-1 M

typing. When you're testing blood type, there are only four possibilities: A, AB, O, and B. PCR on one gene (the DQ-Alpha) can reveal up to twenty-eight types instead of four.

Another process known as Polymarker PCR testing can give a more precise and persuasive answer as it investigates the distinguishing features in five other genes located on five separate chromosomes. (Today, virtually all laboratories use a DQ-Alpha kit that includes Polymarker, producing statistics as high as one in a million. RFLP, of course, can produce figures in the many millions or even billions.)

How does PCR work? The PCR test can take as little as five cells and replicate them millions of times so they can be read. The most frequently used site, the DQ-Alpha, is found on the sixth chromosome. There are at least ten other sites on various genes that can be used in the Polymarker tests.

The DQ-Alpha region consists of an actual gene made up of 242 base pairs and containing ten alleles. The testing kit recognizes six of these alleles, which can appear in various combinations to form a total of twenty-eight genetic types.

Here's a simple analogy. Suppose you own a Ford car that is made in twenty-eight different colors. Many people own Fords, but they may have a different color from yours. PCR DQ-Alpha determines what color Ford you own. Is it the same color as your neighbor's car or a different color? Does your PCR DQ-Alpha gene have the same form as the questioned sample or is it different?

Does it include you as a possible contributor or does it exclude you?

To take the analogy a step further, if a Polymarker test is used, it is comparable to examining not only the color of the Ford but also whether it is a two-door or a four-door, automatic or manual transmission, a coupe or a sedan, and its year. It's that much more precise and discriminating. Neither test, however, is as powerful as RFLP, which would determine the VIN (vehicle identification number) of the car, in addition to the other characteristics.

During the PCR process, heat is used to "unzip" the DNA base pairs and orient them so that the strips point to each other.

Then the temperature is lowered and primers consisting of an essential DNA building block are activated in the solution. These primers identify the two ends of the DQ-Alpha locus and supply the guideposts for where the process should start. An enzyme known as TAQ (isolated from the bacterium *thermus aquaticus*) is activated, and the temperature is raised again. This causes the enzyme to extend the primers across the region, picking up the elemental building blocks along the way so they can bind with their complementary A, T, G, or C on each strand of the unzipped DNA and form two separate, identical strands of new DNA. The process is then repeated over thirty-two cycles. The end result is about four billion new strands of DQ-Alpha, each of which is identical to the one obtained in the forensic sample. In a sense, this process is similar to the one our bodies use to replicate cells so that we grow from zygotes in our mothers' wombs to full-grown adults. And when we are injured by a cut, our bodies make new cells to repair the damage by copying healthy cells. Each cell replicates the other until enough cells are produced to close and heal the wound.

After the PCR replicating process is completed, the next step is to identify which alleles are present. The identifying probes are contained on a membrane that is dipped into the solution containing the amplified DNA. The alleles that are present bind to their complementary probes and cause a blue dot to form at the portion of the membrane that identifies each allele.

The scientist then compares the dots from the forensic sample with the dots from the defendant's blood sample. If they are the same, it's a match. If they differ, the defendant is excluded as a depositor of the sample. Weak dots—those that are not as dark as the blue control—are discounted as unreadable because the scientist can't be sure they really represent DNA. If none of the dots is as bright as the control, the result is inconclusive.

In degraded samples, as long as the bacteria has not affected the DQ-Alpha portion of the DNA, there will be a result. However, a number of complications plagued PCR testing in 1989. It was fortunate that only the RFLP test would be examined in the Castro hearing.

When I prepared for the hearings in the Castro case, I was relatively ignorant of this new science. Shortly before the start of the hearings, Andrew Rossner, Castro's lawyer, came to me and said, "I have no problem representing Castro in the murder case, but I feel inadequate in the area of DNA forensic evidence."

Polymerase Chain Reaction (PCR)

In the PCR process, DNA from small or deteriorated samples (as little as five cells) is amplified millions of times so it can be read.

Heat is used to "unzip" DNA pairs.

The temperature is lowered and primers are introduced that identify the two ends of the DQ-Alpha locus.

The TAQ enzyme is introduced and the temperature is raised. Heat causes the enzyme to extend the TAQ polymerase across the region, duplicating DNA strands, until they total about ten billion new strands.

A membrane containing identifying probes is dipped into amplified DNA. The alleles that are present in the DNA bind with their complementary probes and a blue dot forms on the membrane. The dots are compared with known samples. If they are the same, it's a match.

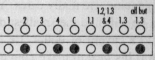

SCHULER

I laughed. "Oh, come on. I'm sure you can handle it," I said blithely. I wasn't an expert on DNA, but I had never run up against any area of the law that was so complicated that it couldn't be mastered with some effort and hard work.

He smiled at my naïveté and urged me to reconsider. "This is tough stuff, Judge. I want to bring in a couple of lawyers for the hearing who know something about DNA testing. Their names are Barry Scheck and Peter Neufeld."

I raised an eyebrow. I knew the men well.

Barry Scheck is an aggressive, irascible street fighter, whose compact body is capable of creating a virtual hurricane of activity in a courtroom. His sharp Brooklyn voice can pierce a witness, and make even bystanders squirm. Most Americans got their first look at Barry in 1995 during the O.J. Simpson trial. I had known him for a long time as a professor at Cardozo Law School, and I'd accepted his invitation to preside over the annual moot-court trials at the law school for many years.

Barry's in-your-face style can be hard to take, but he is a superb advocate. And personally, Barry is charming and genuine. He really cares. You know if he is on your side, he will find the smallest discrepancy and transform it into a cavern of doubt. He has an amazing ability to contort his face to make convincing visual points. Without a word, he displays disgust or shock or disagreement. He poses a question on cross-examination by snarling, and he responds to the answer with a wince, a grimace, or just a sustained stare. Barry is masterful.

Peter Neufeld is tall and curly haired, with the

somewhat distracted but deliberate manner of a professor. He is, however, no less fierce in his advocacy than Barry. Peter had appeared before me frequently when he was a legal-aid defense attorney in the Bronx. I like him and have a great deal of respect for his trial skills. He is perhaps best known for his defense of Marvin Davis, the brother of the notorious Larry Davis, who shot six cops during a stakeout. Marvin Davis's case involved the alleged murder of a pregnant woman. He became a prime suspect when a tissue was recovered from his apartment that (government experts claimed) contained a type of secretion present in pregnant women. Peter fought to have the sample excluded from evidence, maintaining it was based on faulty scientific tests, and he succeeded. The murder charges against Marvin Davis were dismissed.

Scheck and Neufeld had become early authorities in the budding science of forensic DNA. They were a formidable team. But I didn't fully realize that by allowing the pair to handle the Castro hearings I would unleash a massive array of legal talent—and lead to the longest Frye hearing ever conducted—fifteen weeks with five thousand pages of transcript.

A Frye hearing is a preliminary hearing designed to ensure that the scientific evidence the prosecution or defense wants to admit is demonstrably shown to be valid. For example, evidence that is based on an experimental or novel scientific approach cannot be allowed in a trial. The Frye standard demands that a science be sufficiently established for it to be admissible. It also demands that the evidence be properly obtained. For example, if a person is observed weaving in and out of traffic, hits two cars, strikes two people, is stopped, and has alcohol on his breath and shows other signs of drunkenness, one might presume that he is indeed drunk. But if the Breathalyzer test is not conducted properly, the results are not admissible. Whether or not the scientific evidence was admissible would be my decision to make in the Castro case—and I had a lot of learning to do before the hearing.

CHAPTER 4

The Judgment

How can we allow this mess into evidence?
—BARRY SCHECK

The Bronx Criminal Courthouse; March 15, 1989

Before the Castro case, the laboratories involved in DNA testing were a formidable force in criminal cases whose results were often accepted without question. The very first such case in New York, *People v. Wesley,* is a good example.

Like all murders, this one had its own set of terrible twists—most notably the fact that it was a rape-murder of a seventy-nine-year-old woman. George Wesley, a resident of a home for developmentally disabled persons, of which the victim was also a client, was arrested for the murder after investigators found a bloodstained T-shirt with gray and white hairs on it, bloodstained underwear, and bloodstained sweatpants in his apartment.

DNA was not the only evidence. Other trace evidence, along with Wesley's own statements, linked him to the crime.

In preparing to decide whether DNA evidence would be admissible in this case, the court did not even require the lab to perform any testing. The hearing was based strictly on theory. The judge was persuaded and he announced enthusiastically, "DNA fingerprinting—its underlying principles, procedures, and technology—is a scientific test that is reliable and has gained general acceptance in the scientific community. . . ." He went on to say that the technique "will enormously enhance the ability of law enforcement to reduce the number of unsolved crimes that currently occur daily."

In the weeks prior to the Frye hearing for the Castro case, I studied the Wesley decision with care. I was particularly impressed with what seemed to be a foolproof check on DNA-test results: If the tests were not performed correctly, no results would be recorded. The autorads, or X rays, would be blank. I took this to mean that the tests in *Wesley* must have been performed correctly, since there was a result.

As I read about this science, I felt excited about its potential, much as the judge in the *Wesley* case had felt before me. Could it be that, at last, we had found the ultimate test of guilt?

I was filled as well with admiration. If this new science could be used by the criminal justice system, we would be capable of actually proving things that we were once left to surmise.

But I was in for a shock. My first glimmer that this hearing might not be so simple, after all, came when I asked for a list of witnesses. I was staggered by the length of the lists on both sides. Experts piled upon experts. A show of scientific strength unlike any I had ever seen in a preliminary hearing.

On the morning of March 15, 1989, nearly two years

after the murders of Vilma Ponce and her daughter, Natasha, we began the Frye hearing to determine the admissibility of the DNA evidence. Risa Sugarman and Peter Coddington appeared for the prosecution. Barry Scheck and Peter Neufeld appeared for the defense.

Two years seems like a long time to wait for justice. I know it felt interminable to Vilma's family, whose frequent calls to Risa's office were full of rage. They were still certain that Jeff Otero had committed the murders, and they couldn't believe that nothing had been done in these long years to bring him to justice. In spite of Risa's calm and rational certainty that Castro was the killer, Vilma's family continued to demand that Jeff be arrested, and as the months grew into years, they only became more unhappy.

Finally, however, we were about to begin. And the centerpiece would be DNA.

Risa rose and called her first witness to the stand— Dr. Michael Baird, a director at Lifecodes. The direct examination went smoothly. Dr. Baird was clear and confident as he described the RFLP testing process. A man to reckon with in the scientific community, Baird had published many articles about DNA and had testified at a number of trials. His testimony in this one was basically in accordance with what I had read about the science.

With Dr. Baird on the stand, Risa offered into evidence fourteen autorads—or DNA X rays—which demonstrated the results of the tests conducted on the spot of blood found on Castro's watch. The doctor testified that the stain on the watch matched Vilma's DNA.

"What is the possibility that the blood could belong to another person besides Vilma?" Risa asked.

Dr. Baird's reply was stunning: One in 189 million!

"No more questions." Risa smiled and sat down.

"Is there any objection?" I asked the defense, expecting none.

Barry Scheck bounded to his feet. "Your Honor, I'd like permission to conduct a voir dire examination." That meant that he wanted to make sure the autorads had been kept securely, and that they were an accurate representation of the witness's testimony.

This is common procedure to assure that evidence offered really represents what it is supposed to. For example, if a video is offered into evidence that is said to show a sequence of events, but it is determined that the video was edited, it can't be allowed. Barry was doing his job, and doing it well—looking for every potential chink in the state's armor.

As Barry began questioning Dr. Baird, what had seemed like a formality began to grow into a nightmare for the prosecution. One by one, he held up the autorads while he feigned bewilderment. "Something's wrong here," the lawyer said, again and again. Baird was clearly flustered by the attack, and it turns out he had reason to be.

The X rays were mislabeled. They showed the wrong tests performed, the wrong exposure time, the wrong dates, and a whole cascade of sloppy procedures. I sat on the bench and watched with dismay and disbelief. This was a new twist—something I'd never heard of before. I wasn't naive, but like most people, I felt an inherent trust in scientists. I figured that laboratory conditions were above all this. Was I ever wrong!

On redirect, Risa tried to repair the damage by having Dr. Baird refer to his lab notes. But the revelations had obviously caught her off guard. It was a serious problem. The autorads are the most persuasive and comprehensible evidence in the whole DNA process. If they weren't allowed, the DNA case would be worthless.

Slowly and expertly, Barry Scheck and Peter Neufeld dissected the prosecution experts on cross-examination. They demonstrated contamination of important chemicals used to conduct DNA testing, degradation of samples, conscious disregard of scientific protocols, and the inexplicable failure to follow the lab's own guidelines, which it had published in a prestigious journal.

Eventually, Dr. Baird was forced to admit that Lifecodes had used a different scientific method than the one they had described in print—different, too, than the one they had testified to using in other cases.

Barry could not contain his elation. In a moment of sheer exuberance, he raised his arms over his head, like a football referee, and mouthed, "Touchdown!" Some local newspapers covering the hearing had fun recreating that moment for their readers.

Later, Barry stood before me and argued that the errors should bar admission. "There are so many procedural mistakes," he argued, his voice dripping with disgust. "How can we allow this mess into evidence?"

Risa was fighting for the life of her case. She countered that the errors merely affected the weight of the evidence, but should not bar it altogether. "This is good science, Your Honor," she pleaded. "The errors might lessen its weight in the trial, but we should let a jury decide that."

Barry fought back, citing a statute dealing with the admission of X rays in a civil case. "In this case, the errors precluded the admissibility of the X rays," he said. "I submit to you that we have the same situation here."

I recessed court until the next day so I could study the matter and make a determination.

I needed a break, but I wasn't going to get one. The terminology being spouted in my courtroom was like a foreign language to anyone not versed in the science. During the hearing, a friend of mine, a very bright judge, visited my courtroom. I asked him to sit with me on the bench for a while to see if he could understand what the witnesses were talking about. After fifteen minutes, he leaned over and whispered, "I'm leaving. I don't understand one word anyone is saying."

At the beginning of the hearing, I was trying to learn. I stayed up late every night, frantically studying the testimony and not retiring until I could explain it to myself. I remember my wife, Judy, saying to me one night, "Jerry, there are some exciting three-letter words other than DNA."

We both laughed. In fact, Judy understood all too well what I was going through. Judy is my second wife, my soul mate. When we met in 1977, I was a criminal defense attorney and Judy was a family court prosecutor. Now, remarkably, we are both judges. Judy is a tough and dedicated family court judge. Her slight frame and pretty face are deceptive; she is well known for being outspoken and single-minded. She is particularly hard on the out-of-control youths. She will not abide any nonsense in her courtroom. I am a lot more flexible in my courtroom, but together we are a fantastic team. Intelligence, respect, and humor are the hallmarks of our relationship.

We met the day I won an important acquittal in a murder case. I was feeling quite cocky about my victory and decided to celebrate at Peggy Doyle's, a wonderful bar across the street from the courthouse, whose clientele was mostly lawyers and judges. When I arrived, I spotted Mike Pearl, the crime reporter for the *New York Post*, seated at a table with a group of lawyers from family court. He waved me over, and I began entertaining the group with vivid details from the trial and how I had won an acquittal. The other lawyers seemed fascinated with my description of a real murder case before a jury— something they didn't see in family court—and I was in my glory.

Suddenly, one of the lawyers looked past me and smiled. "Oh, here she is at last!" he said, jumping to his feet. I looked up a bit grumpily to see who was interrupting my theatrical moment, and there was Judy— beautiful and vivacious, tiny as a schoolgirl, with the biggest brown eyes I'd ever seen. I was speechless—a rare thing for me. I think I fell in love at first sight.

We stared at each other as she approached the table. She stopped a short distance from me, extended her arm and her index finger as far as it could go, and slowly said in a deep, husky voice, "And, who is *that*?"

I said, "Excuse me, but can you get your finger out of

my face?" It was a real Tracy-Hepburn moment. We married several months later, and she brought her two young children into my household.

We'd been joined at the hip ever since, and I could certainly appreciate Judy's point as she watched me poring over transcripts late into the night. There *were* other pleasures in life besides DNA! But I was obsessed with learning. I was not used to being out of my depth in my own courtroom. I had great pride in my thirty years as a trial lawyer and judge. My usual confidence was not there. I had to get it back. Hard work was the answer. My wife would have to wait.

After a terrific beginning, Risa Sugerman was stunned by the mounting compilation of errors. In her worst nightmares she could not have imagined such sloppiness on the part of the lab. She had placed complete trust in Lifecodes and that trust was now shattered. What began as a routine hearing to establish the authenticity of the evidence was turning into a severe threat to her entire case.

This is the kind of searingly painful moment prosecutors often face. It's painful because, although they have deep respect for the process and the law, and although they know it is the defense's responsibility to hold them to their proof, they cannot control every step of the investigation. A prosecutor has to hope and trust that the detectives on the scene performed their jobs correctly, that evidence was properly gathered, labeled, and tested.

Risa knew in her heart that Joseph Castro had brutally murdered Vilma and Natasha. But she had to prove it to a jury, and how could she do that if the evidence was tainted? "I was furious at Lifecodes," she would say later. "And I was even more angry at Dr. Roberts." Dr. Richard Roberts was the scientist Risa had hired to review the autorads before the hearing. "He said they were okay, and I believed him. But now I had this disaster on my hands."

Risa was also offended by the way Barry and Peter were salivating over the mistakes. "They were loud and abusive—obviously used to getting their way," she said. "I couldn't let them win. I couldn't stand the thought."

But ultimately, it was up to me. I was the one who would burn the midnight oil. A judge's job is to make decisions, but unfortunately we are not magically equipped with the wisdom of Solomon. Even so, I was determined to make sense of the information before me and to maintain control of my courtroom. Some lawyers thought I could be a real type A personality in court, and they didn't mean it as a compliment. But I *had* to be in control. I certainly wasn't going to hand over my court to the lawyers! If a judge doesn't remain in charge, a case can take on a life of its own, moving in its own strange way along an unpredictably bizarre path. When that happens, the process has little to do with justice.

After four hours of intense study, my head throbbed. I was disheartened by the lab's failure to notice its glaring errors. I was beginning to see serious problems that I had not read about in any other cases. Perhaps this new science was not all it was cracked up to be. Perhaps the courts had rushed to judgment, after all, not being as careful as they should have been in evaluating and admitting this evidence.

Eventually, after much study and soul-searching, I concluded that the autorads were admissible. I accepted Risa's contention that the errors should go to weight, not admissibility. But I sensed we were not at the end of the argument.

The ace in the defense's hole—the key to its strategy—was a man named Dr. Eric Lander, who was advising Barry and Peter about the tests. Lander had his doctorate in mathematics from Oxford University and now directed a genetics research laboratory at the Massachusetts Institute of Technology. As he took the stand and began to answer questions, it became abundantly clear to me that this self-taught geneticist from Brooklyn was a brilliant man. Indeed, another prominent scientist once remarked, "Eric Lander is probably one of the five smartest people in the world."

He was also strident and officious—bordering on arrogant. His powerful presence filled the courtroom. I could see that Dr. Lander was not only having a good time as a scientist, he was also relishing his role as a kind of surrogate attorney.

As the defense presented its case, other well-credentialed scientists followed Dr. Lander. Incidentally, this parade of experts contradicts the criticism one often hears that indigent defendants can't get equal justice. At my discretion as judge, I agreed to assign Dr. Lander as an expert and to pay his expenses and those of the other scientists out of public funds. The ultimate cost of the hearing for the defense, paid by the state, was approximately $150,000.

Witness after witness testified for the defense that

DNA testing should not be used in forensic cases because one could not be sure that the samples were clean and substantial. Forensic samples such as blood and semen are usually found on dirty streets, carpets, and wood floors, and in vaginal cavities that are full of bacteria. DNA's use, they suggested, should be restricted to a clinical setting where pristine samples can be assured. Considering the mess that had been presented to me by this sloppy lab, they sure had enough ammunition to argue their position. But even with the holes in the case, I was not yet convinced of the case against forensic DNA. My long nights of study had not been in vain, and I was becoming comfortable with the theory, techniques, and language. Because of that, my disappointment with the testing process of Lifecodes was all the greater.

On the stand, Dr. Lander testified that in the crucial effort to determine if the blood on the watch belonged to Vilma, further testing should have been performed. Without these tests, he told the court, there was no way to scientifically state that the blood was Vilma's.

Here's what had happened. Four tests had been conducted. Three were clear and could be explained, but the fourth was not. Dr. Baird argued that the two bands in question might have been caused by bacteria. Dr. Lander contended that the two extra bands were Vilma's DNA—in which case there would be no match. All the scientists, from both sides, agreed that the blood on the watchband was *not* Castro's. But they disagreed about whether it was Vilma's.

Contaminated samples, probes, or controls are a serious issue in DNA testing because they're capable of

The Disputed Castro Autorad

The autorad in the Castro case showed a three-band match between Vilma's blood and the blood on the watch. However, the two bands at the upper left hand side were unreadable. Were they bacteria or were they Vilma's DNA? The defense argued that if the bands were Vilma's DNA, there would be no match. The prosecution argued that it was definitely bacteria. I had to decide.

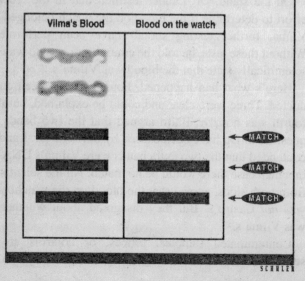

Vilma's Blood	Blood on the watch
	← MATCH
	← MATCH
	← MATCH

producing extra bands on the autorads, and these can cause differences in scientific opinion. That was precisely what was happening here.

Barry Scheck recalled Dr. Baird to the stand and faced him, assuming a posture of disbelief. "Dr. Baird, you've heard Dr. Lander testify that these two extra bands are not bacteria. Do you still insist that they are—that the other scientists are wrong?"

"I believe it's bacteria," Dr. Baird said.

Barry sneered. "Dr. Baird, would you bet your ranch on that?"

There was a moment of silence, then Dr. Baird replied softly, "No."

At the prosecution table, Risa let out a sigh and put her head down. The catastrophe was growing.

What Risa didn't know was that behind the scenes, the scientific experts for the defense and the prosecution were organizing a little mutiny against the prosecution. All, that is, except Dr. Baird.

That evening, they arranged a secret meeting to be held in Dr. Lander's hotel room. There, Lander told the scientists that they needed to reach a consensus about the results of the tests. Over the course of a long evening, the group hammered out a statement, which they all signed. Their focus was the issue of human versus bacterial DNA.

As I took the bench the following morning, I noticed that Barry Scheck was looking particularly cocky. In fact, everyone at the defense table seemed to be smiling. I soon learned why when Barry rose to his feet, waving a sheet of paper. "Your Honor, I offer this into evidence."

I scowled at him. "You offer *what* into evidence?"

Risa was on her feet yelling, "Objection!"

"Sustained." I looked down at Barry. "What the hell is going on here?"

Barry handed copies of the paper to me and to Risa and we read it quickly. I was very surprised, and Risa grew pale. The statement, signed by all of the scientists except Dr. Baird, announced that it was impossible to determine if the DNA was human or bacterial without further testing. Everyone knew that was impossible; the blood had been totally consumed in the previous testing.

"This document is inadmissible. It is rank hearsay," I said sharply. "But you may recall Dr. Lander to the stand. Let's hear about this."

Lander returned to testify about the meeting. Risa was fuming, but clearly she'd lost this round. "I was sand-bagged," she mumbled bitterly. She was dismayed to find that Dr. Richard Roberts, her own highly respected expert, was among those who signed the statement.

The scientists had forced the prosecution into a corner. Risa had to admit in her final argument that the results of the DNA tests designed to show that Vilma's blood was on Castro's watch were probably inadmissible because the additional tests were not conducted. She argued, however, that DNA technology itself was a powerful and reliable test when properly conducted. It was capable of scientifically distinguishing one person's blood from another's. And even if these tests could not establish for certain that Vilma's blood was on the watch, it could clearly exclude Castro himself as the source of the blood. Even the scientists agreed with this point.

Risa was passionate as she urged, "Your Honor, don't throw out the baby with the bathwater. We can admit that the tests in this case didn't rise to the proper level of scientific admissibility. That's the bathwater. It's different from the baby. Don't throw out DNA."

Barry argued heatedly that the mess presented in the name of scientific testing should not be condoned by the judicial system. Clearly, he said, the science had not advanced to the point where it could reliably distinguish one person from another. Even though the test could *exclude* Castro, it could not *include* Vilma.

In the end, it was left to me. Admit the evidence? Exclude the evidence? Or, perhaps, like Solomon, cut the baby in half?

The hearing ended some fifteen weeks after it began, generating a five-thousand-page transcript. Now, with the questions, issues, and errors swirling around me, I set to work formulating my decision. In addition to other factors, as a judge in the Bronx, I also had to consider the type of jury I would have in this case. The typical Bronx jury, I had learned from experience, was composed of the salt of the earth. These people demanded honest evidence and had zero tolerance for mistakes. In spite of Risa's plea to "let the jury decide," it wasn't really that simple. A jury should not be put in the position of having to deal with clear failures in the testing process. It would be ridiculous to have the prosecution and defense agree that the testing was not sufficient to allow an identification by DNA, yet ask me to give these results to a jury and let them try to sort it out. There is, in all cases, a certain minimum standard of reliability and integrity that evidence must meet before it can be admitted.

In constructing my opinion, I tried to be objective and rational, asking myself the questions that seemed fundamental to the issue:

- Is there a body of evidence, generally accepted in the scientific community, that supports the reliability of DNA forensic testing?
- Do techniques or experiments currently exist that are capable of producing reliable results in DNA identification and that are generally accepted in the scientific community?

These were the questions that the Frye hearing had raised. However, I added an additional one before the evidence would be admitted:

- Did the testing laboratory employ accepted scientific methodology in analyzing the forensic samples in this particular case?

This question was designed to ensure that any future mess like the one in *Castro* would first be examined by a judge before submitting the test results to a jury.

To answer the first question, I conducted an extensive study of the issue. There was certainly unanimous agreement that DNA is the fundamental determinant of the genetic characteristics of all life-forms. With the exception of identical twins, individuals differ because of the unique arrangement of their DNA.

In answering the second question, I noted that although DNA testing seems new to us, the techniques and procedures are neither novel nor recent discoveries. For many years, laboratories have used them in conducting DNA analysis in diagnostics, clinical, and research projects. All of the procedures have gained general scientific acceptance. Only when the technology is transferred to DNA forensic identification does it generate dispute.

There's no question that there's a big difference between clinical settings and crime scenes. For example, when scientists do analysis for clinical or diagnostic purposes, they use fresh or dried blood samples from a known source. If an experiment does not yield an interpretable result, they need only return to the source to get more blood and repeat the test with the new samples. In forensic cases, however, the sample—say a bloodstain found at a crime scene, or a semen sample obtained from a rape victim—is limited. If the experiment goes awry, there is no way to redo it if the sample is consumed in the testing process.

I was only obligated to answer the first two questions to make a ruling in the Frye hearing. But I wanted to add another statement—to alert judges who would be dealing with this issue to the promises and pitfalls of forensic DNA. So the third point became an evaluation of whether this particular laboratory, Lifecodes, had performed DNA tests in such a way that the results were tainted.

As I studied the mass of transcripts and reviewed each

stage of the hearing, I reached several conclusions—albeit reluctantly.

The first problem was that Lifecodes had used contaminated probes, and that had very serious implications. Their record keeping was also abysmal. In one of the tests, for example, the control used was from a male scientist who was an employee of the lab. But when the probe for sex determination (DYZ1) was applied, it lit up the female DNA in the female control lane. DYZ1 can identify the Y chromosome, which only exists in the male DNA. How could a male control light up as female DNA?

On the stand, a Lifecodes expert tried to explain this anomaly. He said that the male scientist suffered from a "short Y chromosome" that was mistaken for an X and therefore lit up the female DNA. This was a ludicrous-sounding explanation, and I remember well how Dr. Lander, sitting behind the defense table, laughed silently and mouthed the word "Bullshit." Then the flustered expert tried to explain that the male scientist suffered from a bacterial condition that was literally eating away portions of his Y chromosome, causing the probe to attach to the female DNA. This explanation only added to the absurdity—especially when the expert admitted under Barry's swift cross-examination that anyone suffering from such a condition would be dead! The scientist who donated his DNA was still very much alive.

Finally, the mystery was solved when sloppy lab records were deciphered and it was discovered that the probe was from a female lab employee, not a male.

But the most troublesome issue was the two extra bands on Vilma's lane. The watch lane had only three bands, and these matched with three of Vilma's bands. Were the other two bands bacteria, as Dr. Baird insisted, or were they Vilma's DNA?

In the end, it became clear that the possibility of error was great.[*] There had been too much sloppiness, too many mistakes. While the blood on the watch might well have been Vilma's, the evidence was not sufficient for use in a court of law.

To tell you the truth, the lab's incompetence infuriated me. How dare they come into a courtroom in a double-murder case and offer such careless work? It was an insult to invoke the name of science for such junk. What bothered me most was that it didn't represent the truth. That's what we were there for—to determine the truth. I wanted to make a statement: "Before you introduce evidence into a courtroom, make an effort to assure its integrity."

In the end, I did cut the baby in half. I declared DNA evidence to be a powerful scientific method that could indeed distinguish one person from another. At issue was the manner in which the tests were performed. In order to assure accuracy, the tests must be done correctly. Because most of the experts and the prosecution itself admitted that further tests were required before a reliable result could be obtained, the evidence of a match between Vilma's DNA and the DNA on the watch was not admissible in evidence. However, since DNA testing *is* reliable, the fact that the DNA on the watch was *not* Castro's *could* be admitted into evidence.

[*]It is interesting to note that the same lab and tests were used in the Spencer case, and they went uncriticized. The difference was that Barry and Peter weren't on the defense team.

On August 1, 1989, the day I rendered my decision, the media was out in force. Reporters and TV cameras filled the hallways around my courtroom. The media tended to interpret my decision as a blow to the use of forensic DNA. I didn't see it that way. I believed DNA was an important, even a revolutionary tool. But I would not admit the use of improperly conducted tests' results.

Barry Scheck and Peter Neufeld were successful in their campaign to prevent the introduction of major evidence against Castro. Their role completed, they returned the case to Andrew Rossner, Castro's original lawyer.

Risa was discouraged by the results of the hearing, but she couldn't rest yet. There was one more hearing to go—the Wade hearing. It was designed to make sure that a suspect had been properly identified without police suggestion. Jeff Otero would take the stand to tell his story about seeing Castro in the alley only moments after the murder and his eventual identification of Castro's photo, without police influence or suggestion.

Risa was concerned about how Vilma's family might react to the sight of Jeff on the stand. Before the hearing, she took them aside in the hallway outside the courtroom and whispered urgently, "I just won't have it if you sit in the court and give out vibes that you think Jeff did it." They promised Risa they'd remain mum, but as they filed into the second row of the courtroom, she had her doubts.

She was also nervous about Jeff as a witness. She didn't really know him very well. Shortly after Castro's arrest, he had packed up and moved to Florida, seeking to run from the nightmare of his family's slaughter. He'd only recently returned to the Bronx, and Risa had spoken to him very briefly. She knew, however, that he could blow her whole case, depending on his demeanor and the content of his testimony.

When court was in session, Risa rose. "The prosecution calls Jeffrey Otero."

Jeff shuffled through the cavernous, mahogany-walled courtroom, looking awkward in his dress clothes. His hand shook as he took the oath. Vilma's family stared at him intently.

He sat in the witness chair clutching his hands. His right leg jiggled nervously as Risa began to question him about what he had seen the day of the murders.

As he spoke, Jeff suddenly choked on his words and began sobbing. The courtroom spectators watched in stunned silence as his entire body shook with grief. A break was called to give him time to compose himself. Risa glanced over at Vilma's family. They were visibly tearful and stricken. She knew in that moment they finally believed in Jeff's innocence. Now their anger would be directed at Joseph Castro—where it belonged. Finding no police misconduct, I denied the defense motion to suppress the identification and directed that the case proceed to trial the next day.

In the morning, before jury selection was to begin, Andrew Rossner asked to approach the bench. He and Risa huddled together in front of me. "My client is having second thoughts about going to trial," Rossner said. "He's willing to plead guilty for a sentence of fifteen years to life."

"No way," Risa whispered. "He killed two people."

"She's right," I said. "I can't give a guy fifteen years for two murders. That would be ridiculous." I turned to Risa. "What would be acceptable?"

We spent some time discussing the issue of sentence. Back and forth, between the defense attorney and prosecutor. Finally, I said, "Risa, if you recommend twenty-five years to life concurrent, I would have no problem with that." I knew, as did Risa, that the parole board would be reluctant to release Castro after the minimum time since the crime was so horrible. Risa agreed. So did Castro.

I was pleased that the case was over, but there was one question that still troubled me and occasionally kept me awake at night.

I asked Rossner, "Would your client, during his plea of guilty, agree to answer a question for me?"

He spoke with Castro, and Castro nodded his head yes. After the formalities of the plea were completed, I looked at Castro and asked, "Did you have blood from the deceased on your watch?"

Castro looked me in the eye for a chilling moment, and his mouth twisted in a smirk.

"Yes," he replied.

And so the case ended, and with it came certainty that Joseph Castro was the murderer. Strangely, the lone voice of Dr. Baird, to which no one listened during the hearing, was finally revealed to have spoken the truth. The DNA on the watch *was* Vilma's, and the extra bands, which had caused so much trouble, were indeed bacteria.

This knowledge, however, provided me with little comfort. I had been forced to make a decision without knowing the full truth. When it is quiet and I am alone, a troubling thought occasionally haunts me. I wonder what would have happened if the only real evidence against Castro had been the DNA. When I think about it, I shudder, knowing that my decision to exclude the evidence might have set a brutal killer free to kill again.

CHAPTER 5

Bitter Ends

Didn't you people learn anything from four
months in the courtroom on Castro? How can
you do this to me again?

—RISA SUGARMAN to Dr. Baird

It's my job as a judge to do the right thing—not necessarily what's convenient or popular. I firmly believed
that I had made the right decision in *Castro*. Nevertheless, I was haunted by the debate I had unleashed in the
forensic community. Most frustrating was the media's
misinterpretation of my decision, which led to the belief
that I was an anti-DNA judge. It's hard to describe how
maddening it was to wake up the day after the *Castro*
decision to a banner headline in *The New York Times*:
RELIABILITY OF DNA TESTING CHALLENGED BY JUDGE'S
RULING. And when Barry Scheck told the *Times* he
believed the courts should now review all of the cases
that had relied on DNA, it sent a chill up my spine. I had
a horrifying vision of a Pandora's box of messy paternity
suits, uncertain convictions, and reversals opening up
before my eyes. My greatest fear was that rapists and
murderers would be set free because of erroneous conclusions about DNA testing. I didn't want to be responsible for that. I was anxious for people to understand the

basis for my ruling. And I wanted them to be aware of the importance of DNA science to the future of the criminal justice system.

It's not easy being a judge and having to look beyond the human drama to the law. A judge is not without feelings; I know I'm not. When Joseph Castro looked me in the eye and said yes, the bloodstain on his watch was from Vilma Ponce, I had to consciously control my anger. The pictures of the slaughter in the Knox Place apartment flew into my mind. *He* had done this, taking away those young lives and the life-to-be in Vilma's belly as if they were nothing. One could not be human and feel anything but revulsion. But sitting there on the bench, in the robes that symbolized my dispassion, I did not have the luxury of listening to my own emotions. In the courtroom, the law reigns supreme—even if that means that sometimes a man like Joseph Castro might go free. It was my mandate to follow the law, even when it gave me sleepless nights.

In the weeks following the *Castro* decision, I tried to set aside my deep fears that the decision would be misunderstood and ponder instead the vast implications of this new science. I now counted myself one of the few people in the law who truly understood the nature of DNA testing. The more I studied this new science, the more convinced I became that it was remarkably accurate, *if* the tests were done properly. Unfortunately, that could be a big if.

Invitations to lecture on the subject started pouring in. I accepted each one without hesitation, relishing this opportunity to explain the legal aspects of DNA.

Were DNA test results to be admissible or not? I looked forward to the day, and I knew it would come, when DNA's credibility would be as strong as a fingerprint. Properly tested, DNA was *better* than a fingerprint.

Risa Sugarman would long remember the *Castro* Frye hearings as the worst four months of her life. Still, she believed in the power of forensic DNA, and she wasn't going to let one mistake scare her away from a tool that could bring more criminals to justice.

In fact, even while the *Castro* hearings were taking place, she was trying to solve another case, one equally horrible.

On November 12, 1988, Evelyn A., an eighty-year-old woman, was raped and strangled in her Bronx apartment. As detectives were conducting their investigation, they noticed that the case had similarities to two other rapes that had taken place around that same time. The first victim was Camilla S., a young married woman who woke up in the middle of the night to find a man's body pressing down on her. For an instant, before the reality sank in, she thought she was having a bad dream. The intruder tore at her nightgown and began to rape her, throttling her with strong hands. Before she could get enough air to scream for her husband, who was asleep in another room, she passed out. Fortunately, Camilla survived the attack, but in the dark bedroom, she never saw the face of her assailant.

The next rape occurred when Maria D., a young single woman coming home from work, was grabbed on a Bronx street and raped in a nearby alley. During the attack, Maria caught a brief glimpse of the man's face, but she was too traumatized to offer any real description to the police.

So far, the detectives told Risa, no suspect had been identified. They had samples of sperm from all three victims and a latent fingerprint from the apartment of the eighty-year-old woman. But they had no suspect to link with the evidence. And at the time, they didn't have technology sophisticated enough to match the latent print. The process was done manually, fingerprint card by fingerprint card, an impossible task.

Risa was determined to solve the case nonetheless. "I have an idea," she suggested. "Let's run a DNA test on the sperm collected from the three women and see if it matches. We can at least find out if we're dealing with one perpetrator, and that will be a start."

Risa sent the specimens to Lifecodes and the information came back: it was a match. She now knew that a single person had committed all three rapes and she was dealing with a particularly frightening entity in the community: a serial rapist who was also a killer.

"He's mine now," Risa said when the results were in. "I'm going to get this guy." But who was he? There was not a single clue to help the police track down a suspect.

Then suddenly, in mid-February, the rapes stopped and the trail grew cold. There was no suspect, only a genetic fingerprint that couldn't be matched. The case stayed open and detectives continued to follow every lead. But sadly, they had to resign themselves to the possibility that the case would never be solved.

This was heartbreaking news to the victims and their families. Evelyn's son called nearly every day, hoping for a new lead that would help catch the man who had raped and murdered his elderly mother.

"We have to find him," he said again and again to Risa. "If this animal could do something like that to my mother . . ." His voice shook. "Who would rape an eighty-year-old woman?"

Risa also conducted many interviews with Camilla and Maria, taking them slowly over the events, looking for the tiniest clue. This was a very painful process. When a woman has been raped, the investigation and questioning can sometimes make her feel as if she is being raped all over again. Although Risa was gentle and sensitive in her questioning, the suffering this was causing the women was evident. And neither one could give any details that would lead to a suspect. Maria admitted that maybe she'd seen his face for a second, but it was very fast. Risa could see that Maria was still terrified. The young woman wanted to put this nightmare behind her; she was unwilling to go to the precinct and look at mug shots.

Then, in 1991, long after the verdict in the *Castro* case and nearly three years after the crimes were committed, the FBI introduced a new computerized fingerprinting system, called the State Automated Fingerprint Identification System (SAFIS), that could swiftly compare and identify latent prints. Risa sent the print from Evelyn's apartment for comparison, and it came back showing a clear match with a man who was currently in jail.

Excited, Risa reviewed the information. She couldn't believe they had their man! Henry Caseo, the contributor of the fingerprint, was serving four to twelve years for attempted rape. Perfect. Better still, he'd been arrested on February 16, 1989; that's why the rapes stopped. This result was a long time in coming. The first person Risa called was Evelyn's son.

"Are you sitting down?" she asked.

"You got him!" he yelled.

"Well," Risa cautioned, "it's not certain yet. But we've matched the fingerprint found in your mother's apartment to a guy doing time upstate. We're going to follow it up."

As she hung up the phone, there was a loud roar behind her. For a second, Risa thought all of New York was cheering her good fortune. But it was just the sounds of an afternoon baseball game at Yankee Stadium. Probably one of the Yankee players had hit a home run.

The following day, Risa sent two detectives upstate to interview Caseo. They came back with mixed news. "He confessed to the murder of the old lady, and the rape of the woman in her apartment. But he says he didn't do the street rape."

"Really." Risa looked at the detective doubtfully.

"He says he's got an alibi. He was with his girlfriend."

"Lucky girl," Risa said sarcastically. "Okay, let's talk to her."

It turned out that Caseo's girlfriend was not at all willing to give him an alibi. "He lies about everything," she told Risa. "He wasn't with me that night, and I don't care if I ever see his face again."

His alibi in doubt, investigators returned to Caseo and

pressed him to admit to the third rape. He still maintained his innocence.

"We'll see about that," Risa said confidently. "We've got the DNA." All she needed was to test the semen collected from the victims and see if it matched Caseo's. "Let's send the semen and Caseo's blood sample to Lifecodes," she instructed. Two years after the *Castro* fiasco, Risa had been assured that Lifecodes had cleaned up its act. If they said the semen was a match, she'd believe them. Risa requested and received a court order directing Caseo to give blood. All of the fluids were sent to Lifecodes.

When Lifecodes called to say the tests were completed, Risa arranged to drive up with a detective and her own biologist to review the autorads. She was in good spirits on the drive up the New York Thruway. The lingering gloom of the *Castro* hearing had lifted. She was ready to trust DNA again.

But Risa's good mood didn't last long. As she sat in the lab reviewing the autorads with Mike Baird, a terrible sinking feeling took hold of her. "It was *Castro* all over again," she later recalled. "They were still using that contaminated probe, and there was bacteria on the autorad of the third victim, Maria—the one Caseo hadn't confessed to, the one we most needed to prove." And again, the sample was totally consumed in the testing.

Risa couldn't stand the idea of having to endure a repetition of the *Castro* debacle. She fought to keep her temper in check, but she really wanted to fling the autorads across the room and scream holy hell.

"Didn't you people learn anything from four months in

the courtroom on *Castro*?" she hissed at Baird. "How can you do this to me again?"

Baird tried to explain, but Risa cut him off. "No, doctor, let *me* explain something to *you*. We have three women, one of them dead, the other two marred for life by this man's terrible deeds. Do you know what would happen if the autorad from the third rape were admitted? The case would go down the drain. The defense lawyer would tear us apart. Do you even care? I really wonder."

She stormed out of the lab and gulped in the air outside. This was really intolerable. With the best forensic science ever discovered, this lab couldn't even get its act together. How do you tell rape victims and their families, or the families of murder victims, that you couldn't prosecute because the lab had screwed up?

Risa knew she would have to give up the idea of prosecuting Caseo for Maria's rape. One might think that in the scheme of things, it didn't really matter. If Caseo were convicted of one murder and two rapes, he'd go to prison for life anyway. But it mattered to Risa. For one thing, if she hadn't noticed the contamination and had allowed these autorads to go before a jury, Caseo would have walked on the third rape and the other two cases might have been affected. And even if he was convicted for the murder and two rapes, that was little comfort to Maria, who deserved satisfaction just as much as the other two.

When Risa returned to her office, she picked up the phone and made the call she had been dreading—to Maria—whose rape they'd never be able to prove.

"We can't get Caseo on your rape," she told the shy young woman. "There was a problem with the lab results. But I promise you, we'll get him on the other two and he'll never walk the street again."

The young woman started crying, and Risa thought she detected relief in her voice. Now, at least, she wouldn't have to testify in court.

"Just get him," Maria said. "That's all that matters."

On the first day of Caseo's trial, Evelyn's son appeared in court holding a large photo of his dead mother. When Caseo walked into the courtroom, before the jury was seated, the grieving man spat at him.

"You did it!" he screamed. "You did it!" It gave him some satisfaction to confront the person who had raped and murdered his mother. But it gave him still more when Caseo pleaded guilty. The DNA evidence pointed the finger, and the killer had no choice.

Nevertheless, Risa wouldn't sleep well that night. It had been another close call. At this rate, a disaster was bound to happen. And it did, but this time Risa was not involved in the case. It happened in Portland, Maine.

While Risa was dealing with the problems caused by Lifecodes's sloppy work, Portland deputy district attorney Laurence Gardner was facing an equivalent nightmare. The case involved the prosecution of a man named Kenneth McLeod, who was one of the most dreaded type of criminals—a repeat child molester.

Gardner had anticipated an open-and-shut case. Although he didn't have a great deal of circumstantial evidence linking McLeod to the crimes, he had, he believed, the only real evidence he needed: semen samples taken from the victims. When he sent these, along with a sample of McLeod's blood, to Lifecodes, he was confident that there would be a match. And indeed there was. Gardner had his man, and he looked forward to putting him away for a very long time—long enough so that he would never touch a child again.

But from the moment he stepped into the courtroom for the Frye hearings, a horrified Gardner saw his once-certain case being blown apart.

The trouble began with an important discovery violation. Since the defense planned to argue that the statistical calculations were inadequate, Gardner needed data from Lifecodes to support its findings. When no data was forthcoming as the trial date neared, an exasperated Gardner got in his car and made the daylong drive from Portland to Valhalla. Only when he was actually standing in the offices of Lifecodes was he given the data he needed to argue statistical validity. Unfortunately, it was too late. The court deemed Lifecodes's failure to turn the material over earlier a clear discovery violation and ruled it inadmissible.*

This was a blow to the prosecution, but things only got worse. As occurred in *Castro*, Lifecodes didn't follow its own laboratory procedures. Dr. Baird, once more on the hot seat, frankly admitted this to Gardner. Sizing sheets were undated and uninitialed, making it impossible to

---

*According to the rules of discovery, the prosecution must turn over all relevant materials to the defense well in advance of hearings or trial. If they fail, the material and any testimony—no matter how important—that relates to it may be deemed inadmissible.

account for their accuracy. Worse, the defendant's lane was misidentified on two autorads.

Gardner was depressed by the errors. He had followed the details of the Castro hearing closely, and he couldn't believe that the same lab problems still existed. But it wasn't just sloppiness at work. Horrifyingly, it appeared that Lifecodes had done the most unscientific thing imaginable—rejected or concealed data that did not support its conclusions. They literally hybridized two of the same samples, making the result a complete fabrication. By the time the cross-examination of Dr. Baird was completed on Friday afternoon, Gardner feared that his entire case was going up in smoke.

On Saturday morning, he frantically sought advice from the state's independent expert, Dr. Cal Vary. "Can we salvage this?" he asked the scientist. Vary shook his head glumly.

"There's too much sloppiness," Vary replied. "It's impossible to get independent verification."

Gardner held his head in disbelief. "I found myself in the same position as Risa Sugarman had in *Castro*," he would say later. "My expert prosecution witness was turning into a defense witness before my eyes."

Reluctantly, Gardner decided that it was pointless to continue the hearing. It was like a train running at high speed toward an inevitable disaster: the conclusion that the evidence was hopelessly tainted.

On Monday morning, Gardner stood before the judge and in a trembling voice said, "Your Honor, the state withdraws the evidence."

The judge gazed at Gardner's devastated face and asked quietly, "Does the state withdraw its case against Mr. McLeod?"

Gardner gulped. "Yes, Your Honor."

"Mr. McLeod, you are free to go."

McLeod, accused child molester, let out a whoop of joy. As he made his way out of the courtroom, he didn't pause to thank Dr. Baird, but he might have. Lifecodes had set him free.

Gardner later sent a scathing letter to Lifecodes. "The state will not suffer further by paying for Lifecodes's incompetence," he wrote. "Therefore, do not bother to bill the State of Maine for any additional fees—you will be simply wasting the postage."*

I was deeply disturbed by the growing list of errors. Here we had this fantastic science, this unbelievable ability to finger a criminal beyond all reasonable doubt, but we were forced to submit to mistakes that rendered its data invalid. It was like winning the lottery and losing your ticket.

And other issues were swirling around the scientific community in the wake of *Castro*. The question still remained: if the testing was properly conducted, was forensic DNA a viable proof in a court of law?

---

*In fairness to Lifecodes and Dr. Baird, it must be noted that they have now corrected their procedures. In fact, in a 1995 rape case I handled, the result of their testing was so clean, clear, and compelling that the defense was forced to concede that the DNA profile of the sperm removed from the victim's vaginal cavity matched the defendant. Indeed, the defense now claimed consent, in contrast to their original assertion that the defendant never had intercourse with the victim.

In response to *Castro,* the National Association of Criminal Defense Lawyers (NACDL) established a DNA Task Force in the fall of 1989. The group was led by Barry Scheck and Peter Neufeld, who loudly declared that forensic DNA might be a case of "the emperor having no clothes." I was uncomfortable with this position. My reading on DNA had taught me the opposite: forensic DNA was well dressed and more than presentable for a court of law! Certainly, I understood why defense lawyers might be eager to dismiss the science. It could provide devastating evidence against their clients. But I was anxious to see the issue framed correctly.

The following spring, Barry and Peter would have another chance to hone their skills in defending a client against DNA evidence. The case involved three members of the Cleveland chapter of the Hell's Angels motorcycle gang. Steven Yee, Mark Verdi, and John Bonds were accused of killing David Hartlaub, allegedly because they thought he was a member of a rival gang. Hartlaub was shot inside his van fourteen times with a silenced MAC-10 machine gun.

When typing tests were done on the blood in the van, some of it was determined to be of a type other than Hartlaub's. Perhaps, detectives speculated, a bullet ricocheted and hit one of the suspects. DNA tests were conducted on Hartlaub and all three suspects, and the analysis by the FBI lab showed that some of the blood in the van came from John Bonds.

Barry and Peter launched an aggressive attack on the FBI testing procedures—once again finding a multitude of errors and poor procedures. The prosecution held firm, asserting that in spite of the problems with the testing procedures, there was still virtually no chance that the blood in question came from anyone but Bonds.

Although the court noted that there were "troublesome questions about the quality of the Bureau's work," the results were admitted, and the defendants were ultimately convicted.

Barry and Peter may have been disappointed with the result, but if anything, it heightened their commitment to seeing that forensic DNA was held firmly to the flame of careful scrutiny.

In 1992, three years after the *Castro* decision, the National Research Council published a report by many outstanding scientists, including Dr. Eric Lander, that supported the conclusions I had rendered in *Castro*. The report noted that DNA testing was generally accepted in the scientific community. I was pleased to see this. The third prong of my argument—that labs use accepted methodology in their analyses—had caused the most discussion, conflict, and confusion. That these prominent scientists considered it an important step before receiving DNA into evidence was heartening news.

Many court decisions, not only before but after the publication of the report as well, did not follow this recommendation. In cases where tests were not performed correctly, it was left for the jury to confront the uncertainties. These courts reasoned that if a jury concluded that the tests were not reliable, it was their right to ignore them in their deliberations.

In my opinion, this is a poor way to administer a criminal justice system. While juries are the ultimate finders of fact, it is unacceptable to pass information to them that is clearly unreliable or untrustworthy.

CHAPTER 6

One in a Million

Stop playing games with the truth!
                                    —JUDGE SHEINDLIN

The most heated debate in the forensic community only a few years ago was the use of statistical calculations in the presentation of DNA evidence. When an expert appeared on the witness stand and was asked the statistical probability that the man or woman in the defendant's seat had left the questioned blood, semen, or other sample, the expert's answer would undoubtedly become the focus of intense review in later appeals. Indeed, the question of statistical calculations was the primary focus of the National Research Council's report. Many people believed that the viability of forensic DNA would come down, ultimately, to a game of numbers—a question of odds. This caused great consternation among prosecutors, whose job it is to put away vicious criminals who are almost certainly guilty. They did not like the notion that verdicts might be overturned based on a disagreement about the interpretation of numbers.

A case in point is *Arizona v. Bible*. This was a particularly gruesome case in which DNA, in conjunction with other circumstantial evidence, was used to point the finger at the rapist and murderer of a nine-year-old girl.

In the early summer of 1988, the Jones family was staying in Flagstaff, Arizona, a picturesque and bucolic setting. On the morning of June 6, as the family prepared to visit a ranch about a mile down the road, it was decided that nine-year-old Jennifer would ride her bike to meet the rest of the family in their car. Jennifer started out on her bicycle shortly after 10:30 A.M. The family waved to her as they drove past her on the road.

When the girl had not arrived at the ranch by eleven, her mother began to worry. The family started searching for her and soon discovered her abandoned bicycle by the side of the road. Frantic, they called the police.

Within minutes, the Flagstaff police arrived and began combing the area. During the course of their search, one of the investigators took Jennifer's mother aside.

"Did you see anything unusual or suspicious?" he asked. "Any cars on the road?"

She remembered passing two cars on the way to the ranch. One of them stuck in her mind. "It was a dark-colored Blazer-type car," she told the police. "I saw it twice. Once on the way—then, at the ranch, I saw it speeding in the opposite direction."

"Can you describe the driver?"

She nodded slowly, her uneasiness escalating. "Yes . . . I noticed him. He was a young guy in his twenties—a dark-haired, dark-complexioned white man. He gave me a strange look when he passed us on the road."

In a seemingly unrelated incident, a man in nearby Sheep Hill contacted the Flagstaff police saying he believed his brother had stolen a car. The man told police that his brother, Richard Lynn Bible, had arrived at his house that day driving a Blazer. He'd said the car belonged to a friend, but his brother suspected that it was stolen.

When police received a description of the vehicle, they immediately thought there might be a connection between this incident and Jennifer's disappearance. Soon they learned that a GMC Jimmy with a damaged rear fender was missing from the impound lot.

Richard Lynn Bible was spotted driving the car near a wooded area around 6:30 P.M., and a high-speed chase ensued. When police finally cornered him, Bible ran from the vehicle and hid, but he was soon located and taken into custody.

Bible admitted that he had stolen the vehicle and repainted it, but he vigorously denied any knowledge of the missing girl.

Since the car had once been used for newspaper deliveries, police found a large quantity of rubber bands in the rear. They also noticed a case of Suntory vodka in the vehicle, two bottles of which were missing. In the ashtray was a Dutch Master cigar along with its crumpled band and wrapper. Packets of Carnation Rich hot chocolate were also found. Finally, there were spatters of blood. When he was captured, Bible was wearing a blood-stained shirt with tobacco residue in the pocket.

Three weeks later, Jennifer's body, wrapped in a sheet, was discovered in a field. Surrounding the body were numerous rubber bands; later, it was determined that they matched the rubber bands found in the car. As police spread out across the area looking for clues, they found a stubbed-out Dutch Master cigar, which was forensically determined to be similar to the one found in the Jimmy's ashtray, and which also matched the tobacco residue in Bible's shirt pocket.

As they followed the trail of evidence, police found an empty ten-pack of Carnation Rich hot chocolate packets. Farther along, they discovered two empty Suntory vodka bottles.

Pieces of metal found near the body exactly fit the damaged portion of the car and another piece of metal previously retrieved from it.

An autopsy revealed that Jennifer had suffered multiple blows to the skull and a broken jawbone. Although her body was naked and her hands tied, suggesting sexual molestation, no semen was found.

This was a case in which the circumstantial evidence was overwhelming. But the verdict would ultimately depend on minute fiber and blood evidence. Piece by piece, the damning evidence mounted:

- Hair retrieved from Bible's shirt was found to be similar to the child's hair.
- Hair of the youngster was also found in the car and on a blanket inside it.
- Hair similar to Bible's was found on the sheet covering the body and on the victim's T-shirt.
- A lock of the victim's hair pulled from her head and found near the body was tangled with a pubic hair determined to be similar to Bible's.
- Fibers attached to this lock of hair were determined to be similar to the lining of the jacket Bible was wearing when he was arrested.

- Fibers found near Jennifer's body were forensically determined to be from the car's seat cover.
- Additional fibers found at the scene and on the shoelaces used to tie Jennifer's hands were identified as coming from Bible's jacket lining.
- Other fibers recovered on the scene were connected to the green blanket found in the car.

DNA tests compared the blood found on Bible's shirt to Jennifer's DNA and found them to match—with a margin of error of one in sixty million, and potentially as great as one in fourteen billion.

In April 1990, Richard Lynn Bible was convicted of first-degree murder, kidnapping, and molestation of a child under the age of fifteen. He was sentenced to death, but his conviction was reversed. The appellate court determined that the statistical calculations used in testimony about DNA were not scientifically accurate and thus created an unfair prejudice against the defendant.

This reversal stunned the prosecutors in the case. There were so many pieces of evidence linking Bible to the crime. How could such a thing happen? It all boils down to a confusion about the use of DNA testing.

When they present DNA evidence in court, scientific experts always state statistical probabilities. That *seems* to make sense. After all, the difference between one in a thousand and one in a billion is enormous. But how are the statistics computed?

Here's an example. Assume that four DNA tests are performed on four different sections of chromosomes, and a match is found between the DNA sample left at the crime scene and the defendant's DNA. The next step is to compare the four separate DNA matches to four separate databases consisting of a large number of randomly chosen people whose DNA was previously profiled. In the case of the FBI, this database currently consists of Black, Hispanic, Southeastern Hispanic, Southwestern Hispanic, Caucasian, and Asian populations.

The bands are compared to the database. If one other person out of five hundred tested has the same-length DNA at one area of the chromosome, the statistical probability is one in five hundred. The process continues until all of the bands are compared. The figures are then multiplied (i.e., $500 \times 500 \times 350 \times 400$), producing fantastic numbers. If, for example, you have a Caucasian defendant, the expert would give the opinion that the odds of finding another person in the Caucasian population with the same-length DNA bands is one in thirty-five billion.

For some time now, a debate has raged in the scientific community about the validity of this statistical analysis, and the opposing positions have made their way into the courtroom—which is why you see cases reversed on the basis of statistical calculations. One school of scientists claims that there are subpopulations that are not reflected in the laboratory database. They argue, for instance, that the gene pool for Italians in the Caucasian database may not be the same as the gene pool for Scandinavians. And they note that although Hispanics from Puerto Rico may have a different gene pool than Hispanics from Spain or South America, these groups are lumped together as "Hispanics."

Another school of scientists argues that its research reveals very little distinction among the populations tested. Indeed, they find the variations to be so small that even if the database were adjusted to account for them, the ultimate odds would still be phenomenal. Their premise is that the argument over statistics is more academic than relevant in a courtroom.

After long study of the matter, I reached the conclusion that the use of statistics in a criminal case is simply mischievous. A trial is supposed to be a search for the truth under the rules of evidence. Therefore, the most meaningful question presented to a scientific expert should be: "Is this the defendant's DNA within a reasonable degree of scientific certainty?" That's the legal language that we've always used in presenting expert opinions. Why not with DNA?

It's interesting that such confusions are rarely allowed to surface in paternity cases. The expert might say, "This man is the father, and there is a 99.9 percent probability of that fact." The expert doesn't offer the odds of anyone else being the father, although there is a faint statistical possibility. It is not deemed relevant.

Another example. In a case involving fingerprinting, the opinion might cite statistics showing the chance of anyone else leaving that print other than the defendant to be one in 200 million, as there are only approximately 200 million fingerprints on file. Does this mean that two people out of 400 million have the same prints? Probably not. It just means that the fingerprints of every person in the world are not on file.

Here's a simple way to get your mind around the issue. Let's say the question is, "Am I six feet tall?" One can safely say that I am less than one mile high, although that statement is not very meaningful to the issue. One might say I am more than one inch high, but again that's not very meaningful. However, if the opinion is that I am less than eight feet tall, the evidence is closer to the truth we are seeking. If the evidence shows that I am more than five feet tall and less than eight feet, that is also closer to the truth. To get what we accept as an accurate answer, I would be compared with other randomly selected people, or be measured by an accepted standard, say of feet or meters.

Should not the same rules of evidence be applied to DNA forensic science? Rather than a confusing and meaningless statistical analysis, I believe the questioning of scientific experts should go something like this:

Q: Can you state with a reasonable degree of scientific certainty whether the genetic material recovered is consistent with the defendant's genetic makeup?

A: Yes.

Q: What is your opinion?

A: The defendant's genetic makeup is consistent with the genetic makeup of the sample recovered at the scene.

Q: What is the basis of your opinion?

A: It would be an extremely rare occurrence for anyone other than the defendant to have the same genetic makeup as that found in the sample.

This is closer to the truth we are seeking in a court of law. It does not confuse. It is not wildly speculative. Of course, this assumes we're looking for the truth. Unfortunately, that's not always the case.

Another conviction in an extremely bloody murder case was also challenged on the basis of statistics, although this one had an interesting twist.

Carla Almeida was a twenty-one-year-old new mother employed as a masseuse at Andre's Massage in Meriden, Connecticut. The morning of April 18, 1988, started like most others. Carla rose early and drove her live-in boyfriend, Gerard Patano, to his job in her Volkswagen van. She then drove their infant son to the home of her aunt for day care. She planned to return for Gerard around five in the afternoon, and to pick up their son by 5:30. But she failed to arrive for either pickup—and her family never saw her again.

At 2:00 P.M., Michael Sivri called Andre's Massage, requesting that a masseuse be sent to his home. For safety purposes, the company asked him to supply his name, address, and telephone number, and informed him that he would be required to show the masseuse photographic identification when she arrived.

After servicing her second customer of the day, Carla telephoned Andre's and was told that Sivri would be her next customer for a one-hour massage.

Andre's had a strict policy that required its employees to call in at the beginning and end of each appointment. Carla called when she had arrived at Sivri's home and checked his identification. But when she had not called

Andre's after a couple of hours, and they were unable to get a response from Sivri's phone, they called the police.

Lieutenant Henry DiJulio and Officer James Arlio of the Trumbull Police Department were dispatched to drive by Sivri's residence and see if anything was amiss. No one was there. Both Carla's Volkswagen and Sivri's truck were gone.

Carla's unoccupied car was later found.

When Sivri returned home, the police were waiting. When they questioned him, he readily admitted, "She was here. She gave me a massage, I paid her, and she left."

Suspecting foul play, the police obtained a search warrant and notified Sivri that his home would be searched three days later. They were accompanied by Dr. Henry Lee, a prominent forensic scientist and director of the Connecticut State Forensic Laboratory.

Henry Lee is a colorful character, known as one of the best forensic "detectives" in the world. He has investigated some five thousand murders. Born in China, Lee was a police officer in Taiwan before coming to the United States. His voice is rich with the accent of his native land, and his eyes dance with intelligence and humor. Lee often testifies at criminal trials, usually for the prosecution, and juries are drawn by his warmth and honesty. He is particularly expert in crime-scene investigation and the interpretation of blood-spatter patterns.

Sivri was not home when the search took place.

Bloodstains and splatter were found in Sivri's home. There was also human tissue in the garbage can in the garage and blood droplets leading from the house to the

garage. On the wall of the family room were smears that
appeared to come from someone trying to wipe away
blood.

Dr. Lee noticed that the carpet in the family room was
damp and discolored. It appeared to have been rubbed
with a liquid containing soap. He carefully cut a portion
of the carpet, exposing its underside and padding. There
he discovered a huge amount of fresh red blood. It had
apparently saturated the surface of the carpet, seeping
through to the underside and soaking the padding underneath. Dr. Lee speculated the victim had lost at least two
pints.

Tests showed that it was human blood, although there
was no way to match it with Carla's, since no body had
been discovered.

Dr. Lee was also able to evaluate the pattern of blood
splattering throughout the premises to demonstrate that a
mechanical force was used to project the blood in small,
randomly distributed patterns.

By now the police were very interested in talking to
Sivri further. But on the day his home was to be searched,
he quit his job and left for Turkey, explaining vaguely to
friends at work that he had "personal problems."

Several days after fleeing the country, Sivri's abandoned truck, without plates, was discovered. There was
blood on the steering wheel, floor of the trunk, interior
panels of the truck, and on the rear bumper. The carpet
had been removed, and inside the truck police found a
bag containing Pine Sol and two unused sponges.

The evidence was mounting. There was only one
problem. No body. Sivri himself might never have been

caught had he not returned to the United States. Attempting to use an alias, he was arrested by the FBI three months after Carla's disappearance.

Investigators had a tremendous amount of evidence leading to the conclusion that Sivri had committed some kind of crime—probably murder.

- Carla was never seen or heard from again after she kept an appointment at Sivri's home.
- Carla's Volkswagen was found abandoned after it had been seen in Sivri's driveway.
- Enough blood was found in Sivri's home to indicate violence had been committed.
- Henry Lee was able to demonstrate that the blood-spatter pattern was consistent with the projectile of a metal object.
- Hair belonging to Carla was obtained from a hairbrush in her home and compared with hair found in the carpet. It produced a match.
- Blood was found in Sivri's abandoned truck.
- Sivri fled the United States and returned using an alias.

Still, no body, weapon, or direct evidence was ever found.

The police began to make the DNA connection by testing both of Carla's parents. When the DNA profile of the blood in Sivri's home was compared with the parents' blood, it was conclusively established that the blood on Sivri's carpet came from the child of those two people.

Sivri was convicted of the murder, but his conviction

was overturned by the appellate court because of a disagreement about the use of statistics. A new trial was ordered.

Sivri might have gone unpunished, but between the first and second trials, a skeleton was discovered not far from where Sivri's truck had been found. Since there was no fluid left, it was impossible to conduct DNA testing, but there was an obvious fracture to the skull, a blunt trauma, supporting Dr. Lee's theory of the murder. Because the jaw and the teeth were intact, a forensic dentist was able to examine X rays that had been taken of Carla's mouth when she was alive. They matched perfectly. Carla corroborated the DNA tests from beyond the grave.

In 1995, Sivri was convicted a second time, and this time the conviction stood.

But because of a debate about the use of statistics in presenting DNA evidence, he might have gone free. It's a disturbing thought.

Another debate in the forensic community concerns the use of the term "match" to describe the autorad results. Technically, the bands are not precisely the same. But if the measures show them to have no greater than a 2.5 percent variation from each other, they are considered to be a match. In the courtroom, this slight discrepancy causes defense attorneys to howl with dismay.

It has been my belief that in our quest for truth in the courtroom, the word "match" is an accurate description of the scientific process—even if it represents a more difficult position for the defense. We sometimes seem to bend over backward to achieve a specious "fairness" that dramatically reduces the power of the DNA tests.

In the case of Henry Hummert, the Arizona Court of Appeals once again challenged the entire idea of a DNA match.

This was a rape case, as ugly and despicable as a case could be. The rape occurred in July 1989, in Tempe, Arizona. Susan M. was returning home from a party at 3:30 A.M., and was leaving her car when she was surprised by a male assailant. He pressed a handgun against her temple and, holding her tightly, forced her into the yard of a nearby house. He then made her partially disrobe, and he raped her twice.

In all likelihood, the assailant then planned to kill Susan. He grabbed her tightly around the throat and began to choke her, but she bit him on the forearm and he drew back in pain. Furious now, the assailant struck Susan on the back of the head with his gun, causing severe scalp lacerations. Warning her not to move, he hurried to a nearby car and sped away.

Susan stumbled to her feet and ran into her house, where she called police. During the interview, she gave them a general description of her assailant. In spite of her trauma, Susan recalled details about the car he was driving, a red Honda CRX with a gray out-of-state license plate with black lettering on it, bearing the numbers 939. She also remembered seeing an emblem on the rear bumper shaped like a map of Texas.

By chance, the next morning, Susan's cousin spotted a red Honda CRX in the parking lot of a fast-food restaurant, and she called the police. When they arrived at the scene, the detectives agreed that the car matched Susan's description, right down to the emblem of Texas and the three numbers. They went into the restaurant and learned that the owner of the car, Henry Hummert, was a manager there.

Hummert was cooperative and well mannered. He assured the officers that he didn't mind answering questions about his whereabouts the night before. He said he'd been with several of his coworkers at a party near the restaurant, and didn't leave until after 4:00 A.M.

As the police listened to Hummert's story, they noticed that he had scratch marks and a puncture wound on his forearm and they asked him about it.

"Oh, that," he answered casually. "I burned myself when I was cooking with hot grease."

The officers then questioned the three coworkers whom Hummert had said were with him the night before, and all three confirmed that he had left the party after 4:00 A.M. (They would later admit that Hummert had asked them to lie; in fact, he'd departed between 2:00 and 2:30 A.M.)

The case against Hummert was solidified when DNA testing on semen recovered from Susan's vagina proved to match his DNA. Hummert was tried and convicted of rape.

On appeal, however, the court once again faced a challenge concerning the definition of a "match." During the trial, Lawrence Pressley, the FBI lab's DNA expert, testified that he could conclusively identify a match between Hummert's DNA and the DNA in the semen sample. He stated that the possibility of a random match was extremely rare, and that the only other person who might have the same DNA would be Hummert's identical twin.

The court of appeals ruled that Pressley's testimony should never have been allowed, and that his description "overstated the significance of the DNA test results." The court agreed that the evidence calling the results a "match" was improperly admitted.

This result is a real shame, in my opinion. Isn't it all so much semantics that clouds the real facts? Is there a reasonable possibility that any other human being on earth besides Henry Hummert committed that rape? Not really.

Once again, the solution is probably quite simple: just ask the expert if he can say, with a reasonable degree of scientific certainty, that the samples match. Stop playing games with the truth.

In any event, by 1994, most genetic scientists were in agreement that "the DNA wars are finally over." Even Dr. Lander supported the conclusion that the argument over population statistics and match probabilities was scientifically settled. The NRC recommended a "ceiling principle," which amounts to the most conservative rendering of figures. Even this conservative standard, however, approximates statistical certainty when four or more chromosomes are matched.

That might have ended the debate. But defense attorneys were not yet ready to concede the supremacy of DNA. It was simply too devastating to their clients.

CHAPTER 7

The Silent Witness

We have the potential within our grasp of a technology that in routine investigations will identify suspects as reliably as fingerprints.

—JEREMY TRAVIS
Director, National Institute of Justice

The case of the Palo Verde tree convinced me, as no other case had, that DNA is a remarkable forensic science.

Caterpillar manufacturing was using a remote area of the Arizona desert to test its machinery. It was called the Caterpillar Proving Grounds.

Early Sunday morning, May 3, 1992, young Tim Faulkner was riding his dirt bike in the secluded area. As he traveled through the dry brush near the intersection of Jack Rabbit Trail Drive and Indian School Road, he was startled to see the body of a nude woman, lying facedown near a cluster of Palo Verde trees. His first thought was that she was dead.

Faulkner sped home, trembling and crying, and his parents called the police. Sheriffs arrived on the scene and the area was roped off as criminologists pored over every inch of ground.

The woman, later identified as Denise Johnson, had been strangled to death, and fresh blood on her body indicated that her death was recent. Matted grass a few feet away suggested the victim had been dragged to her final resting place. A cloth was tied around her neck and left wrist. A shoelace was tied around her left ankle, and a braided wire, attached to a metal ring, was wrapped around her right wrist and ankle. A vinyl strap and another braided wire lay loosely across her neck. The killer had gone to a lot of trouble. He hadn't just strangled her, he'd tortured her.

As the police combed the area, a man who identified himself as Chad Gilliam approached them, saying he had been driving home from a party about 1:30 that morning when he saw a vehicle exiting the Caterpillar Proving Grounds. The vehicle was a white "dually" pickup truck—a heavy-duty vehicle with four wheels on the rear axle—with amber clearing lights on the top of the cab. "The pickup was going pretty quick," Gilliam told investigators. "It ran a stop sign and turned south on Jack Rabbit Trail."

Continuing their search the police discovered a pager lying just a few feet from Denise's body. Upon investigation, it was found to be registered to a man named Earl Bogan. He would tell police that the pager was used by his son, Alan.

Charlie Norton was the homicide detective assigned to the case. He quickly began to track the meager leads, and learned that Alan Bogan owned a "dually" that matched Gilliam's description. He hurriedly got a court order to have the truck seized and searched by detectives. In the bed of the truck, they found no apparent evidence of a crime, but they did find two seed pods from a tree. They seized the seeds as evidence.

Alan Bogan lived about eighteen minutes from the proving grounds with his girlfriend, Rebecca Franklin. Several days after the body was discovered, Detective Norton visited Rebecca and asked her questions about the night of the murder. She told him that Alan had been drinking heavily in their apartment. She left the apartment about 8:30 P.M. to visit a friend, and when she returned three hours later, Alan was gone.

At about 2:00 A.M., Rebecca told Norton, Alan woke her up. She immediately noticed that he had scratches on his face that had not been there earlier in the evening. He explained that he'd been in a fight at a bar. She also told Norton that Alan kept a length of braided wire in his truck.

"Can you describe it?" he asked.

"Yes. It has a small metal ring attached to the end of it."

That sounded exactly like the wire that was found on the dead body. Norton called the station to find out if such a wire had been discovered in Bogan's truck, and he was told no.

Alan Bogan was taken into custody. Under questioning, he admitted to Norton that he had lied to Rebecca about being in a bar fight.

"I see." Norton regarded the young man implacably. "What really happened, then?"

Norton was amazed at Bogan's reply. "I was driving around," he said, "and I picked up a woman who was hitchhiking."

"Okay." Norton breathed deeply. "Can you describe the woman to me?"

As Bogan gave a detailed description of the hitchhiker,

Norton felt the hairs stand up on the back of his neck. He had just described Denise Johnson!

"What happened next?" Norton asked, careful not to betray his excitement.

"We had sex in the truck," Bogan told him. "Then we were just driving and we got into an argument about something—I can't remember what. I stopped the truck and told her to get out. She swiped my pager, my wallet, and some other stuff off the dashboard and ran away. I chased her down, and we fought over my property. That's when she scratched me. I thought I got all my stuff back, but the next day I noticed my pager was missing."

"Where were you when this happened?"

"I don't know. Somewhere out on the highway."

"Not on the Caterpillar grounds?"

Bogan insisted he'd been nowhere near the Caterpillar Proving Grounds. "I haven't been there in years. And I didn't kill that girl."

By this point Norton felt, with the instinct of an experienced detective, that Bogan was lying. Although a good deal of circumstantial evidence pointed to Bogan, Norton thought he needed some more direct way to tie him to the crime.

Norton's colleagues considered him extremely bright and somewhat unconventional—a kind of modern-day Sherlock Holmes. Now he had a hunch. He'd noticed a fresh abrasion on one of the branches of the Palo Verde tree under which Denise's body had been found. He wondered if the seed pods found in the bed of Bogan's truck might be from this tree. Was there any way to match the pods with the exact tree from which they fell? If he could prove the pods came from the tree at the murder site, he could prove Bogan's truck had been there.

It was an incredible long shot, but Norton knew something about the subject of DNA. It was present in all living things, not just humans. Maybe individual trees had a genetic signature, too.

Norton put in a call to Dr. Timothy Helentjaris, a professor of molecular biology at the University of Arizona.

"I have a strange question," the detective said. "Is there any way to use DNA technology to prove which tree some seeds came from? I want to know if these seeds came from the Palo Verde tree at the scene of the homicide."

This was an interesting challenge for the biologist. He knew that human DNA was unique. Was tree DNA unique as well?

"Let me see what I can do," he told Norton.

Dr. Helentjaris used a technique known as Randomly Amplified Polymorphic DNA—or RAPD—to compare the DNA from the seed pods with the DNA from the Palo Verde tree at the scene of the crime. He also discovered that twelve varieties of Palo Verde tree grew in the desert area, and at least nineteen others across the country, and he gathered samples from each one. Then he tested each DNA sample and compared it with the pods found in Bogan's truck.

He found that each of the twelve samples had distinctive DNA; like humans, the Palo Verde trees were quite unique in their DNA patterns.

To assure the integrity of the test, Dr. Helentjaris did it blind. He did not know at the time of the testing which sample came from the tree at the crime scene. He concluded that only one Palo Verde tree of all those sampled matched the seed pods found in Bogan's truck. It was the tree at the crime scene.

"You're not going to believe this," Helentjaris told Norton when he called him many weeks later. "I've got an exact match on the tree."

"Meaning. . . ?" Norton still wasn't sure this was the answer he needed.

"Meaning I am scientifically certain that the pods you gave me could not have come from any other tree in the country except the one at the murder site."

Norton was stunned. "Doctor, you're a hero!" he shouted. This was the proof he'd wanted so badly.

Alan Bogan was convicted of the murder of Denise Johnson, based on a catalog of circumstantial evidence—including the rare seed of the Palo Verde tree.[*]

What a remarkable story! The evidence that sent Bogan away was hidden in the Palo Verde seed, proving that DNA really is the stuff of all life—not just human life. Its importance as a clue in crime solving is sometimes nothing short of miraculous.

In spite of the mistakes that plagued DNA testing during the early years of its use, it has gained currency in

---

[*]If this case is appealed, the outcome is uncertain because the Arizona Supreme Court has been reluctant to accept statistical testimony. Indeed, it has reversed many convictions where the statistical numbers were deemed to be too high, despite overwhelming evidence of guilt.

America's courtrooms as the silent witness to some of the most horrible crimes. Blood evidence usually is, in the terminology of the law, "circumstantial." That is, it is not the "direct" evidence of an eyewitness or a confession. Since most heinous crimes are committed in secret, prosecutors depend on circumstantial evidence most of the time to make their cases. DNA is as close as we've ever come to an actual eyewitness—and in many respects it's more reliable. This science does not lie.

Lay people invariably misunderstand circumstantial evidence and thus, juries often have trouble with it. In real life, people use the word "circumstantial" to mean casual, secondary, and inferior. But in a criminal case, circumstantial evidence, including DNA, can be powerful and certain. It is frequently the vital link between the defendant and the crime.

Here is an example of circumstantial evidence, as it might be explained by a judge to a jury. Suppose you look out your window at 11:00 P.M. and the night is clear and cold. The stars are shining and the moon is out. You retire to bed and awake the next morning at 8:00 A.M. You look out the window, the sun is high, and you see a winter wonderland. All the trees, the street, the cars, and the homes are covered in snow. You did not see it snow, but there it is. If someone asked you if it snowed between the hours of 11:00 P.M. and 8:00 A.M., you would say yes without hesitating. You would have complete confidence in your answer, relying on the *circumstantial evidence* of snow on the ground.

Direct evidence, on the other hand, would be, "I saw it snowing." Obviously, in this case, the circumstantial evidence is just as powerful as the direct evidence. You didn't have to see it snow to know that it had snowed.

Here's another example. Suppose you put two empty milk bottles in the milk box along with a note to the milkman: "Leave two quarts and your bill." You retire to bed and the next morning you open your door and observe that it has snowed during the night. You see footprints leading from the street to the milk box, and another set of footprints leading back to the street. You open the milk box and find two full quarts of milk along with a bill.

Could you conclude that the milkman took the empty bottles, received your note, and left two full bottles and the bill? You did not see him or his milk truck or his milk bottles. The observation of the milk bottles, the bill, and the tracks in the snow are direct evidence. The conclusion that the milkman came, walked to the box, left the milk and bill, and returned to his truck is based on powerful pieces of circumstantial evidence. The inference they lead you to make is strong and reliable. Therefore, you can confidently say, "The milkman was here."

Circumstantial evidence is often the only evidence that exists, since criminals don't normally commit crimes in Macy's window. But neither direct nor circumstantial evidence is always reliable. In life, there are many situations that are foggy and complex. For example, suppose two people are in a closed room and a gunshot is heard. The police break into the room and see one of the people kneeling over a dead body and a gun on the floor. The windows are locked from the inside. The gun has been recently fired, and the smell of gun smoke fills the air. The deceased has been shot in the back. Could you conclude that the person kneeling over the body was the shooter?

Suppose the gunshot was in the deceased's right temple or in another location consistent with a self-inflicted wound? Suppose only the deceased's fingerprints were on the gun? Suppose the second person had made prior threats against the deceased? Suppose the deceased had talked about committing suicide? Suppose the gun was owned by the deceased? Or the defendant? Suppose the window was open? There are many questions that may or may not be answered by direct or circumstantial evidence.

Let's be clear about the role DNA evidence plays in the courtroom. It's not magical. DNA tends to corroborate other evidence. It can serve several purposes in a criminal investigation.

DNA is evidence that can powerfully connect an individual defendant with a crime. On February 26, 1993, a bomb exploded in the underground parking garage of New York City's World Trade Center, signaling the advent of international terrorism on U.S. soil. The massive explosion killed six people and injured thousands.

It would later be determined that two men were responsible for the bombing—Mohammad Salameh and Nidal Ayyad. Ayyad was a naturalized U.S. citizen who had been in the country for eight years. He was a graduate of Rutgers University and lived with his pregnant wife in New Jersey. When he and Salameh met, the two men found that they had much in common; both were from Israel's West Bank. They became fast friends.

Evidence would eventually show that Salameh rented a yellow Ford van, filled it with 1200 to 1500 pounds of explosives, and drove it to the underground garage of the World Trade Center. He set the timing device and left. In the immediate aftermath of the explosion, investigators feared that any vital clues would be hopelessly buried in the rubble of the garage.

On March 3, as investigators continued to sort through the debris, an anonymous letter arrived at *The New York Times* taking responsibility for the bombing. The letter was bold and clear: the bombing, it said, was in retaliation for U.S. support of Israel. It concluded with a warning that future violence was to come. Although the letter was viewed as an important piece of evidence, it did not establish a connection to any specific group or individual, or provide a break in the case. That was accomplished by the folly of Salameh himself.

Investigators on the scene quickly determined where the blast originated in the garage, and they found pieces of yellow metal belonging to a vehicle that they believed to have been a delivery van. By tracing the VIN number imprinted on a large piece of metal, they were led to a rental agency in New Jersey, where they found the name and address of the renter, Mohammad Salameh. Confirming the observation that although defendants are presumed to be innocent, they are not necessarily presumed to be intelligent, Salameh returned to the rental agency on March 4, claiming that the van had been stolen and asking for the return of his $400 deposit. He was immediately arrested.

The arrest of Salameh led investigators to Ayyad, and

he was arrested on March 10. However, prosecutors were concerned that the evidence against Ayyad was far less compelling than what they had on Salameh. They couldn't connect Ayyad with the rental van or place him on the scene. Although it was established that Ayyad had ordered bomb-making equipment and chemicals that were delivered to Salameh's storage shed, possessed a timing device suitable for use in a bomb, and shared a bank account with Salameh, they knew that this might not be enough to prove beyond a reasonable doubt that Ayyad was actually involved in the bombing.

DNA was the critical link. The investigators turned their attention to the letter that had been sent to *The New York Times*, analyzing it for any identifying clues. Since DNA is present in saliva, they used PCR DQ-Alpha to test the sealing surface of the envelope and found that it had indeed been licked before closing. Following a hunch, they then tested Salameh and Ayyad. The saliva on the envelope was declared to be a genetic match with the DNA profile of Ayyad. Although the PCR test produced the limited statistical likelihood of only one in fifty, combined with the other evidence it was enough for the jury. They found Ayyad guilty.

Another example of DNA evidence being used to connect a suspect with a crime occurred in the case of *Indiana v. Hopkins*. In 1985, Gerald Hopkins was working as an aerobic-exercise instructor at the local YMCA, where he made the acquaintance of Isabelle F., a young married woman. They became friends and Hopkins occasionally visited her at her home.

One night, Isabelle's husband arrived home from work

to find the house in complete disarray and the contents of Isabelle's purse dumped on the floor. He found his wife's nude body kneeling over the bed. Her throat had been cut almost to the point of decapitation.

The coroner later recovered semen from Isabelle's vagina, and reported that she had been raped before the murder. The semen was preserved for testing.

Gerald Hopkins was a suspect in the case. An eyewitness, an acquaintance of Hopkins's, put him near the scene around the time of the murder. He told police that Hopkins ran up to him on the street, looking scratched, nervous, and disheveled. Hopkins blurted out, "Goddamn, nothing went right. I fucked up. That bitch!"

His friend was alarmed. "What are you talking about, man?"

Hopkins grabbed his shirt. "I think they saw me. I got to get out of town. Do you have a gun? Can you take me out of town?"

His friend pulled loose from Hopkins's grip and backed away. "Sorry, man . . ."

Hopkins ran down the street and disappeared. He later managed to flee the area and was not apprehended for three years. During that time the semen recovered from the victim's body was preserved.

It's interesting to note that DNA testing was not yet available at the time of the murder. By 1988, however, when police arrested Hopkins, it was frequently used in forensic work. It's a good thing, because semen was the only real evidence that police had against Hopkins. The semen was tested and it matched Hopkins's DNA. He was convicted of murder.

DNA can place the defendant at the scene. If a suspect leaves DNA at the scene of a crime, it is as powerful as a fingerprint or an eyewitness. In the *Caseo* case, semen was collected from the victims that matched (at least, in two cases) Caseo's DNA. He had left a genetic calling card.

In another case, *Connecticut v. Zollo*, the culprit was identified, thanks to DNA, even though the victim had been unable to identify him. Here's what happened.

Zollo entered the home of his estranged wife wearing a ski mask. He grabbed her at knifepoint, put a bag over her head, wrapped her head in duct tape, and proceeded to sexually assault her for an hour and a half. Remarkably, she didn't realize her attacker was her ex-husband. However, he had left behind a towel stained with his semen.

Soon after the incident, the police received evidence that led them to strongly suspect Zollo in the attack. Most notably, Zollo had told a friend that he was going to get revenge on his wife because she had initiated their separation. He even asked his friend if he'd go with him to rape his wife! The friend refused, but he later told the police what had occurred.

A court order was obtained directing Zollo to give a sample of his blood, and this was sent, along with the semen-stained towel, to the FBI laboratory. RFLP tests showed that Zollo was the contributor of the semen, and he was convicted for the rape. The semen on the towel proved beyond a reasonable doubt that Zollo had been in the apartment.

DNA can identify the victim. Sometimes victims are not known, or their corpses have deteriorated to a point where they cannot be recognized. DNA can help to identify them. Such was the case in *Missouri v. Davis*, where DNA solved the mystery although a body was never found.

On May 4, 1985, Miriam Davis, the mother of two young children, left her office at 5:00 P.M. as she did every weekday, climbed into her red Volkswagen, and drove away. She was never seen again.

The previous weeks had been traumatic for Miriam, culminating in the night she finally called the police, terrified that her husband, Tim, was going to beat her to death. A concerned police officer persuaded Miriam to press charges against Tim, and he was arrested for spousal abuse. For most of their marriage, Tim controlled his wife with violence. Miriam had grown inured to the sudden rages, the black eyes, the scrapes and bruises that patterned her arms and legs. But she had finally reached the breaking point.

When Tim was released on bail, Miriam sought an order of protection against him. She was determined to keep away from him for good. She desperately wanted to put an end to the violence for her own sake and the sake of her young children, Robbie and Angela, who did not deserve to suffer the scars of an abusive homelife.

The order of protection only enraged Tim further. Angrily, he declared to a friend, "The only way to stop a whoring bitch like that is to shoot her." He also told another friend, "If she don't stop messing with me, I'm going to blow her away." To back up his threats, he purchased a twelve-gauge shotgun at a local sporting-goods store.

The day after Miriam disappeared, Tim, unbeknownst to authorities or to anyone else, drove her red Volkswagen to a neighboring town and rented an indoor storage space. He purchased two new locks for the car's doors, and two air fresheners, which he placed inside. He explained to the owner of the storage facility that he was hiding the car to avoid losing it in a divorce proceeding.

When Miriam failed to return after several days, Tim somberly told Robbie and Angela that their mother had abandoned them. He told the same story to the police. Police investigators didn't believe him. They suspected foul play. For one thing, it simply did not make sense that Miriam, a loving and responsible mother, would give up her job and abandon her children, leaving them alone with the man who had caused them so much suffering. For another thing, there was plenty of reason to suspect that Tim, with his history of spousal abuse, was involved in her disappearance. It was not an uncommon scenario. All of the trails led to Tim. There was motive. There was intent. But there was no other evidence.

As the weeks went by with no sign of Miriam or the car, the police reluctantly faced the fact that they could not charge Tim. Without a body or even a sighting of the Volkswagen, there was no legal proof that Miriam hadn't simply turned her back on her family and run away. While the mystery of his wife's disappearance remained unsolved, Tim proceeded to fraudulently empty his wife's bank account, tamper with her insurance policy to name himself as the beneficiary, and obtain a divorce along with custody of the children. Because Miriam had always been gainfully employed, Tim even got a judicial order requiring her to pay child support—if she was ever found.

Three years passed. Miriam's trail was cold. Life went on for Robbie and Angela without their mother. Then Tim made a silly mistake—the kind of mistake that is amazingly common among criminals who often suffer from the fatal flaw of arrogance. He stopped paying the storage charges for the Volkswagen and failed to respond to repeated dunning notices. Finally, the storage space was forcibly opened and a sickening stench filled the air.

This was the break the police had been waiting for and had long since given up hope of getting. But when they pried open the locks on the car, they did not find Miriam's body. Only unidentifiable debris littered the trunk of the car—smears of dried blood, tissue, and a couple of bone fragments. Investigators were certain that these were vital clues to Miriam's demise, but without her body they could not prove it. As shocking and compelling as their discovery was, there was virtually no way they could follow such a meager trail to Miriam.

Or was there? That's where the forensic DNA came in. Since the police had no sample of Miriam's DNA to use as a reference, they could not match the blood and tissues that way. But perhaps the mystery could be solved through Robbie and Angela. A child's DNA is composed of a combination of the mother's DNA and the father's DNA. Indeed, DNA tests are frequently used to establish paternity. Why not *maternity*?

Investigators took blood samples from Robbie and Angela and compared them with the DNA profile of the dried blood found in the car. It was determined that there was a 99 percent certainty that the dried blood scraped from the inside of the Volkswagen's trunk came from the mother of Robbie and Angela.

The mystery was solved by the miracle of science. Tim was convicted of the murder of his wife, even though Miriam's body was never found.[*]

DNA can establish the scene of the crime. Blood or semen recovered from a scene can be linked to a defendant, thereby placing him at the scene. This occurred in the case of *Illinois v. Stremmel.*

Stremmel and the victim, David Burns, attended Alcoholics Anonymous meetings together, but on the night of the murder they were seen drinking together at several bars. Burns was later found at his home lying in a pool of blood. The autopsy determined that death was caused by a severe beating inflicted with a blunt instrument— possibly a tire iron.

There were no eyewitnesses, fingerprints, or evidence of forced entry. The only evidence was a set of bloody footprints that were determined to match the size and style of Stremmel's shoes. The footprints, coupled with eyewitness testimony that Stremmel was the last person

---

[*]You might wonder how a murderer could be convicted without the *corpus delecti*. It is commonly believed that "corpus" refers to an actual body—that a murder can't be proved without a body. But actually, *corpus delecti* refers to "the body of the crime"—the elements that prove it was committed.

seen with the victim, were sufficient to gain search warrants for Stremmel's home and car.

When investigators searched Stremmel's car, they found that the tire iron was missing; a blue contact lens was recovered near the passenger seat; a tiny bloodstain was found on the brake pedal, and a small bloodstain was on the driver's seat.

Burns was wearing only one blue contact lens at the time of his death, and the lens recovered from Stremmel's car was consistent with this lens.

DNA testing of the blood on the brake pedal and the stain on the driver's seat was consistent with Burns, but not with Stremmel. Stremmel's car was proved, by DNA as well as other evidence, to be the scene of the crime.

DNA can identify the place or places where the victim might have been. The case of *Nebraska v. Houser* concerned the murder of a thirty-four-year-old woman. Her boyfriend, Frank Houser, was convicted on the basis of DNA evidence.

On the day in question, the young woman was last seen driving to Houser's home. Several hours later, Houser phoned her parents and asked them if they knew where their daughter was.

"She was at my house, and she left to go to the grocery store and never came back," he told them.

The next day, when their daughter had still not been heard from, the alarmed parents called the police. The latter soon located her car, about four blocks from Houser's home. In it were her purse and shoes. A huge pool of blood, a large sheet of plastic, and a bloody hammer were found in the trunk.

Houser was immediately a suspect, but investigators needed to make a forensic link. They searched Houser's home and could find no signs of a struggle or any clear evidence of blood. They did, however, seize sections of the carpet and pillows that showed unclear stains. Blood was extracted from these items, but who the blood had come from was yet to be determined.

When the body of the victim was finally recovered, it was so badly decomposed that DNA testing could not be performed. To determine if the carpet and pillow blood matched the victim, investigators tested her parents and obtained a match. This was proof that the victim had been in Houser's apartment and had spilled blood there.[*]

DNA can distinguish between "copycat" and serial crimes. You'll remember that the very first use of forensic DNA made this distinction. In the British "blooding" case, Alec Jeffreys was able to assure investigators beyond any doubt that they were dealing with one murderer, not two.

In the case of *Caseo*, it was important to establish whether the murder and rapes were the work of one man or several. DNA testing of the semen established that there was a single perpetrator.

DNA can be the sole evidence that excludes the defendant as the perpetrator. Don't forget that one of

---

[*]Houser's conviction was later overturned because the appellate court ruled that the prosecution had not established a proper foundation for this "extremely technical evidence." There was no preliminary hearing; the evidence was presented for the first time in the presence of the jury—a big mistake, in my opinion.

the most powerful uses of DNA is to *exclude* a person as the perpetrator of the crime. That's the task of the Innocence Project, headed by Barry Scheck and Peter Neufeld. There have been several dramatic DNA-linked reversals in recent years. One was the case of Ronald Cotton, a young North Carolina man convicted in 1984 of two rapes. All along, he denied committing the crimes, and it was true that the evidence that had convicted him was scanty: one of the women identified Cotton in a photo array; that was it. But in 1992, Cotton's new team of lawyers began talking to their client about the possibility that DNA tests might clear him. They warned him, however, that if he was guilty, the tests would show that, too. He gave them the go-ahead, and tests of the semen collected from the victims showed that Cotton could not have committed the rapes. He was freed after eleven years in prison.

In another case, Scheck and Neufeld proved the innocence of a Virginia man, convicted of rape, who had been in jail for more than ten years. Edward W. Honaker claimed his innocence throughout, and in fact, there was very little evidence against him. His fate was undoubtedly sealed by the dramatic courtroom testimony of the victim, who pointed to him as the rapist.

A decade later, Honaker's case came to the attention of the Innocence Project. When Honaker was convicted, DNA testing did not exist. Now Scheck and Neufeld took the vaginal swab containing semen recovered from the victim, and sent it to a lab for genetic testing. The result proved that the semen could not have come from Honaker.[*]

DNA, however, rarely provides the sole evidence to support the conviction of a defendant. The case involving a man named Michael Weeks provides an example.

In the fall of 1991, Carrie R. was a seventh grader in the town of Townsend, Montana. She lived with her mother, two brothers, and her stepfather, Michael Weeks. They seemed to be a normal, happy family, but in December of that year, Carrie was found to be pregnant.

A concerned teacher at Carrie's school made a report to the Montana Department of Social Services, and Cheryl Rolfe, a social worker, came to the school and interviewed the girl.

Frightened and traumatized, Carrie admitted that her stepfather had been sexually abusing her since she was eight years old. She said that the incidents usually occurred two or three times a week, in the morning, after her mother had left for work and before her brothers awakened. In a trembling voice, Carrie said Weeks must be the father of her child. She had never had sex with anyone else.

Cheryl arranged for the girl to be taken from her home and placed in a facility for unwed mothers. The social worker told Carrie's mother that neither she nor Weeks should attempt to contact the girl. But they managed one phone call. Carrie later said that her mother and Weeks phoned her one evening and begged her to change her

---

*Remarkably, it took more than a year for Honaker to receive justice. In the law-and-order state of Virginia, officials are reluctant to set people free—even when the evidence seems so unquestionable. Honaker finally obtained his release late in 1994.

statement and say that someone else was the father of the child.

By the time Carrie gave birth in late July, Weeks was busily preparing another scenario. He denied that he'd had sexual intercourse with his stepdaughter and boasted that he had evidence her brother might be the father of the child.

Blood samples were collected from Carrie, her baby, Weeks, and her brother, and sent to Genelex, a genetic testing laboratory in Seattle. Howard Coleman, the president of Genelex, testified that Carrie's brother could not be the father of the baby, but Michael Weeks could—and likely was. The jury agreed, and convicted Weeks of sexual intercourse without consent. His conviction was affirmed on appeal.

In this case, DNA served as almost the sole factor in a conviction. But in the great majority of cases, some other evidence points to the defendant. As every experienced detective knows, criminals rarely escape without leaving some clues to their deeds.

In 1994, a trial involving DNA would shake the very foundations of the science. Like everything else about the O.J. Simpson case, DNA would be swept into a maelstrom of confusion. For those who believed this was a make-or-break case for DNA—and I was among them— it would prove torturously frustrating and loaded with mixed messages that would plague us for a long time.

CHAPTER 8

Brentwood Butchery

> You see what they're trying to do? They're trying
> to mislead and confuse the jury. Don't let that
> happen, your honor.
>
> —PROSECUTOR MARCIA CLARK

San Francisco; July 1994

As Alameda County prosecutor Rockne Harmon took his daily run around Lake Merritt, his thoughts were two hundred miles away in Los Angeles. He'd just learned that he had been tapped by Los Angeles district attorney Gil Garcetti to play a key role in presenting DNA evidence in the trial of O.J. Simpson. It was already being called the case of the century—the one that would establish once and for all the credibility of forensic DNA.

That may or may not have been true. But the Simpson case, months before the start of the trial, was quickly gaining unprecedented notoriety. Football legend O.J. Simpson was charged with the brutal slashing murders of his ex-wife Nicole Brown Simpson and her friend Ronald Goldman. The case, according to prosecutors, would hinge on the substantial blood evidence. To argue this portion of their case, they were prepared to go outside Los Angeles to get two of the best DNA prosecutors in the country—Harmon and his San Diego colleague, prosecutor George "Woody" Clark.

"They want you down there," Harmon's boss, DA Jack Meehan, had told him the previous day. "I agreed, but I warned them about you. They should know that there's very little *give* to your approach."

Harmon smiled. The handsome forty-nine-year-old prosecutor, named after the legendary football coach Knute Rockne, was widely regarded as brilliant but prickly and uncompromising. His sharp tongue often got him into trouble both in the courtroom and at the many conferences where he enjoyed going head-to-head with DNA naysayers. Harmon was a pro, but he had a hard time not taking his cases personally, and he was outspoken when he felt the courts had made a mistake.

Harmon had been smarting ever since the California appeals court made a ruling two years earlier that challenged the admissibility of DNA. The appeal consolidated two unrelated cases in which convictions were based on DNA evidence.

The first case involved Ralph Edward Barney, who was accused of kidnapping, raping, and robbing a woman at gunpoint. A DNA comparison by Cellmark Laboratory of semen recovered immediately following the crime matched Barney with a probability of one in 7.8 million in the African American population, and the jury convicted him based on the DNA evidence.

In the second case, Kevin O'Neal Howard strangled and beat to death his landlord, Octavia Matthews, who had begun eviction proceedings against him for nonpayment of rent. At the time of his arrest, Howard had a fresh cut on one of his fingers. A DNA comparison by the FBI of blood samples recovered from the crime scene matched Howard's with a probability of one in 200 million in the African American population. Howard was also convicted.

The joint appeal challenged the validity of the statistics. The court held that there was no general scientific acceptance of the process of statistical analysis.

The decision, written by First District Court of Appeals justice Ming Chin, infuriated Harmon. He wondered when the courts were going to get with the program. As a result of the Barney decision, the high courts in California were reluctant to put a firm stamp of approval on the admissibility of DNA statistics.

If Harmon occasionally let his frustration spill over when discussing the California courts, he felt his anger was justifiable. Whatever anyone might say about his raw temper and sharp tongue, Harmon was quick to remind people that he wasn't the bad guy. "The worst thing a human being can do is done long before I get involved with a case," he would say. "My job is to make sure they are held accountable for it."

Now, as Harmon prepared to go to Los Angeles, he knew that this case would be the trial by fire of DNA evidence. He was well aware that the defense's powerful team of Peter Neufeld and Barry Scheck would try to poke holes wherever they could—claiming that DNA science was too new, too untried, that laboratories were prone to error, that statistics were misleading. It would be his and Woody Clark's job to keep the jury's eye on the science.

* * *

Meanwhile, in Los Angeles, Deputy District Attorney Marcia Clark sat in her cramped office staring tiredly at a stack of juror questionnaires that had been filled out by people in the jury pool. They were of unprecedented length and detail—80 pages and 294 questions, some of them requiring essay-length answers. She had never seen anything like it. Part of the reason was the defense's use of a skilled scientific jury expert. The selection of juries, especially in high-profile cases, had evolved into an intricate psychological chess game. The questionnaires showed that. Many of the questions seemed to bear no relationship to the issues at hand. For example, "Have you ever written a letter to the editor of a newspaper or magazine?" Or, more obscurely, "Have you or anyone close to you undergone an amniocentesis?"

As she always had, Marcia tried to ignore the media hype that surrounds any high-profile case—and especially this one—and zero in like a laser on the true issue: the horrible, bloody murder of two innocent young people. While the rest of the world focused on Simpson, it was her job to keep the victims' faces before the jury—to never let anyone forget why they were there in that courtroom.

Her passion and ferocity on behalf of victims was one of Marcia's trademarks. Like Risa Sugarman, she felt an abiding responsibility to speak out for those who no longer could. Some people criticized her for being strident, but she thought that was ridiculous and unfair. Her job demanded it. If anything cried out for stridency, it was prosecuting murderers. Before the Simpson case, Marcia was best known for winning a conviction against

Robert John Bardo for the stalker slaying of young Hollywood actress Rebecca Schaeffer. Rebecca's family spoke often with gratitude about Clark's dedication and the way she kept in close personal touch with them throughout the trial, making them a part of her team. Her aim was justice, and she had been their pillar of strength.

The murder of Nicole Brown Simpson and Ronald Goldman had all the earmarks of a modern-day soap opera: the ghastly slaying of a beautiful young woman, the ex-wife of a famous football hero, and her young, handsome male friend. A history of spousal violence, drugs, and acrimony that could be traced back to the start of the Simpson marriage. A reportedly jealous Simpson, who stalked his ex-wife and was known to be bitter over their breakup. And finally, a mountain of circumstantial evidence linking Simpson to the crime.

The murders occurred on a balmy June night in Brentwood, a wealthy suburb of Los Angeles. In the small dark courtyard of Nicole's condominium, a scene of violence occurred, sometime between 10:00 and 11:00 P.M. Remarkably, no one in the neighborhood heard a sound. There were apparently no screams. In the end, Nicole was left with her neck slashed so deeply that the spinal column was visible. Her head was nearly severed from her body. Ron Goldman, a friend who had stopped by on an errand, had been cornered near the back gate where he had no chance of escape or self-defense. He was stabbed many times; several of the wounds were fatal. Both victims were found lying in large pools of blood. It was a crime that bespoke great rage.

Within a week of the terrible events, O.J. Simpson was

in a jail cell, charged with the murders, and Marcia Clark was heading up a team of prosecutors whose job would be to prove his guilt beyond a reasonable doubt. It seemed like a tall order for the slender, attractive woman with the huge doelike eyes. But Marcia was tough as nails and brilliant in the courtroom.

It was somewhat ironic that Marcia was leading this case. Before the murders, she hadn't even known who O.J. Simpson was! When Detective Phillip Vannatter had called her early in the morning of June 13 to report a double homicide and ask her help getting a search warrant, she was surprised to hear the location. "It sounds like a pretty tony address for this kind of thing," she said.

"Marcia," Vannatter replied, "it's O.J. Simpson."

"Who's that?" Marcia asked sleepily.

"The football player . . . *Naked Gun* . . ."

"I'm sorry," Marcia said. "I don't know him."

But she knew him now—perhaps better than she ever wanted to know another human being.

Based on the evidence, Marcia had a detailed theory of what had occurred on that terrible night.

On the day of the murders, Simpson and Nicole had attended a dance recital for their daughter, Sydney. They were barely civil to one another; Nicole clearly did not want anything to do with her ex-husband. She did not save him a seat at the recital, nor did she invite him to a family dinner at a nearby restaurant after the event.

Nicole, her parents, sister, and two children spent a pleasant evening at the Mezzaluna restaurant, then returned to their homes. Sometime later, Nicole received a call from her mother saying she had dropped her glasses in the restaurant parking lot. Nicole called the restaurant and the glasses were retrieved. Ron Goldman, a young waiter and a friend of Nicole's, offered to drop the glasses at her condo after he left work.

Meanwhile, Marcia speculated, Simpson was in a state of rage over Nicole's rejection. Shortly after 9:30 P.M., he drove his white Bronco the short distance to Nicole's condominium, wearing dark clothes, a dark cap, leather gloves, and carrying a knife. He may have planned to kill Nicole, or he may have only intended to slash her tires—something he'd done before.

Simpson, Marcia believed, was hiding in the bushes behind Nicole's building when Ron Goldman arrived to return the glasses. His fury spilled over at seeing Nicole with another man. He leaped from the bushes, striking Nicole with such force that she fell to the ground, unconscious. Then he pushed the surprised Ron Goldman up against the gate, forcing him into a position from which there was literally no chance of escape, and stabbed him again and again until the young man fell dead. During the slaying, the knife slipped and cut Simpson on the hand. Somehow, the cap was pulled from his head, and one of the gloves fell to the ground.

Finally, Simpson returned to the injured Nicole, pulled her head up by the hair, and slashed her throat.

Marcia believed that Simpson then ran from the scene, leaving a trail of bloody footprints, and quickly drove the short distance to his Rockingham estate. He climbed a fence in the back, accidentally dropping the second glove, and ran through the dark yard into his house, leaving drops of blood along the pathway. A pair of bloody socks later found in Simpson's bedroom would bear witness to his haste.

The timing was of great importance, since Simpson was scheduled to leave for a trip to Chicago that evening. The testimony of Alan Parks, the limo driver who arrived to pick him up at 10:40 P.M. and found no one at home, would be essential testimony in the prosecution's case.

Marcia felt the theory was solid. While domestic violence was still a tough sell in the courtroom, and tougher still when the perpetrator was a beloved celebrity, she knew in her heart, and by virtue of the evidence, that the road to these murders was paved with many years of abuse and spousal terrorism. She also knew that a history of violence would not be enough to convict Simpson. The key would be the results of the DNA tests, which she hoped would provide the irrefutable link between Simpson and the murders. Now she concentrated on the sections of the jury questionnaires dealing with DNA. It was vital that the jurors who were eventually seated were willing and able to comprehend the complex DNA evidence.

She had been there before. In 1991, Marcia had prosecuted a man named Christopher Johnson for murdering a male friend. The case was especially tricky since the dead man's body was never found. But a single spot of blood was recovered from the rear passenger seat of Johnson's car. By comparing the DNA profile of the blood spot with the DNA profiles of the missing man's parents, Clark had been able to get a match. She won a conviction based on this small piece of evidence.

Now she could not help but think if one drop of blood

could be so convincing, surely an entire blood trail would be as well. If only the jury could see it that way.

Marcia brushed a lock of curly hair from her eye and lit a cigarette. The portion of the juror questionnaire relating to DNA evidence yielded little information. The questions seemed vague and stilted on the page:

The ability of DNA analysis to prove the identity of the person(s) whose blood or hair is found at a crime scene has been the subject of some television and radio shows, and magazine and newspaper articles. The following questions pertain to the subject.

Before the Simpson case, did you read any book, articles or magazines concerning DNA analysis? Yes?   No?

If yes, please name the book, magazine, newspaper or other periodical where you read about it and briefly describe what you recall having read.

Are you aware of any other court cases involving DNA analysis?   Yes?   No?

What is your view concerning the reliability of the DNA analysis to accurately identify a person as the possible source of blood or hair found at a crime scene? Very reliable?   Not very reliable?   Somewhat reliable?   Unreliable?   Don't know? Please explain your answer.

Have you followed any of the court hearings concerning DNA analysis in the Simpson case? Yes?   No?

What are your views concerning what you have heard and/or read about the DNA hearings in the Simpson case?

The answers circled on the questionnaires didn't really satisfy Clark. The truth was, no matter what a juror said on a questionnaire, there was no way to predict how he or she would respond in the actual setting of the courtroom. And for the most part, the questionnaires revealed that potential jurors knew very little about DNA at all. Even if someone had heard about the science, few people were capable of evaluating it. That would be her job in the courtroom, and she knew from past experience that it was no easy task.

When I learned that the Simpson case would be based on DNA evidence, it sparked my attention. By that time, I was well known as the "DNA judge." I was eager to see the science used in a setting that would be instructive to the public. And surely this was such a case. I was struck by how much this case resembled many that had been argued in my courtroom. For example, the fact that Simpson had a cut on his hand was so common to knife slayings. Remember Castro's cut on his hand? Blood is slippery, and when you're stabbing furiously and causing massive flows of blood, it's not unusual for the knife to slip and cut you, too. And while the media would make much of the absence of witnesses and the failure to recover a weapon, these details did not bother me terribly. Murderers choose the time and setting for their crimes, and they rarely perform them in public. I thought there was plenty of circumstantial evidence in this case, but much would hinge on the jury's understanding of DNA.

As Rock Harmon and Woody Clark began to review the evidence, both experts agreed that it was strong. They were accustomed to far less—perhaps a spot of blood or a smear of semen. This was a virtual cornucopia—a blood trail consisting of many samples, all of them a match with Simpson and the two victims. They reassured Marcia Clark that the evidence was compelling. And as the results from three different labs began to trickle in, the evidence appeared to be some of the strongest any of the prosecutors had ever seen. Among the early results:

1. Blood found on the Bronco instrument panel matched Simpson. (PCR)
2. Blood found on the Bronco's center console matched Simpson. (PCR)
3. Blood found on the Bronco's driver's side wall matched Simpson. (PCR)
4. Blood found on the Bronco's carpet matched Nicole Brown Simpson. (PCR)
5. Blood on the right-hand glove found at Simpson's residence matched Ronald Goldman. (RFLP and PCR)
6. Blood on a sock found in Simpson's bedroom matched Nicole and Simpson. (RFLP, PCR)

7. Blood on a second sock found in Simpson's bedroom matched Nicole. (PCR)

8. A drop of blood near the victims' bodies matched Simpson. (PCR)

9. Blood on the walkway leading away from the victims matched Simpson. (PCR)

10. Blood on the rear gate at the Bundy Drive crime scene matched Simpson. (PCR)

11. Blood on the driveway at Simpson's home matched Simpson. (PCR)

The courtroom arguments would hinge on two different perceptions of the truth about the DNA evidence: the prosecution's position that it proved that no other person on the face of the earth could have committed these crimes; and the defense's contention that the evidence was tainted, contaminated, and possibly planted by police.

As they prepared to argue, Rock Harmon tried not to be cocky. Long experience had taught him that a trial could take on a life of its own, that evidence, once clear and compelling, could turn murky and questionable under the close scrutiny of the defense.

By the time DNA made its entrance into the packed Los Angeles courtroom, the trial had already been under way for more than three months. The pretrial hearings had been lengthy. The lawyers in the case were already tired, and so was the jury. Marcia worried about that. She glanced often into the solemn faces of the jurors, as if willing them to stay alert, to really listen to the DNA evidence.[*] This part of the trial lacked the visceral drama of the earlier testimony, but it was more significant than anything they would hear. She prayed they were up to the task.

On May 8, 1995, the prosecution began its DNA case, with Woody Clark calling to the stand Dr. Robin Cotton, the laboratory director of Cellmark, one of three labs to which the prosecution had sent samples. Dr. Cotton's rather daunting task was to introduce the lay jury to the complicated world of DNA science.

She was well suited for the job. Smiling and soft-spoken, wearing oversized glasses, Cotton looked like a high-school biology teacher. She already had performed the task of teaching juries around the country about DNA some ninety times. Most observers found her likable and trustworthy in the courtroom, a professional with no ax to grind.

Addressing her comments directly to the jury, Cotton began to methodically define the meaning of DNA. She used simple examples from real life and basic science, demonstrating how each person's DNA, the result of a pairing of two parents, was utterly unique. She explained in the simplest terms possible the methods her laboratory

---

[*]Shortly before the pretrial hearing was scheduled to determine the admissibility of DNA, the defense told Judge Ito that it was willing to waive the hearing and allow the evidence to be presented directly to the jury. Ito agreed, probably to save time, but I believe it was a mistake to skip the hearing. As I wrote in the *Castro* decision, the DNA hearing is an essential part of the process. It guarantees some agreement among the parties before evidence is presented to the jury. Without a hearing, the jury is left to sift through the controversies that will surely ensue. While that might have served the defense ends of confusing and creating doubt in the eyes of the jurors, it was not good courtroom practice.

used to test blood, saliva, semen, or other bodily fluids to isolate and identify the DNA.

After Dr. Cotton laid the groundwork, the prosecution began the slow task of linking O.J. Simpson to the crime.

Testifying day after day in her unflappable manner, Cotton focused on four pieces of evidence: a blood drop from the foyer of Simpson's Rockingham home, a blood drop from the Bundy Drive crime scene, a blood drop found on Ronald Goldman's shoe, and a bloody sock recovered from Simpson's bedroom.

She said the blood drop lifted from Simpson's foyer contained DNA with the same distinctive series of genetic markers as Simpson's blood.

A sock found at the foot of Simpson's bed tested positive for blood, and Cellmark's analysis of DNA extracted from the sock showed that the blood could have come from Nicole Simpson.[*] O.J. Simpson and Goldman were excluded as possible DNA "donors."

Although blood on the bottom of Goldman's shoe was difficult to analyze, Cotton testified that several genetic markers were consistent with Nicole Simpson's blood—perhaps demonstrating that Nicole was already bleeding before Goldman was killed.

Cotton said a sample of Simpson's blood, in a spot on the Bundy crime-scene walkway and in blood from the foyer of Simpson's Rockingham home, was extremely rare.

---

[*] In lay terms, we'd call it a "match," but Judge Ito did not allow the word "match" to be used to describe DNA evidence—even when the statistical likelihood was as much as one in nine billion.

"The odds that blood found at the scene of the murder could have come from anyone but Simpson are about one in 170 million," Cotton said, looking straight at the jury and pausing to let the magnitude of the numbers sink in. Furthermore, Cotton said, the blood found on Simpson's sock and identified as Nicole Brown Simpson's had DNA characteristics matched by approximately one in 9.7 billion Caucasians. Her meaning was clear. Since there were only five billion people on earth, Nicole was the only person in the world with that match.

With the jury mulling over the dramatic statistics, Peter Neufeld approached his cross-examination cautiously. There are only so many ways a defense team can legitimately challenge such compelling DNA evidence. The most obvious strategy is to plant confusion in the jurors' minds about the validity of the science, the reliability of the statistical calculations, and the potential for error or contamination. Scheck and Neufeld were masters of that art. When I heard they were joining the Simpson defense team, I knew that these men's skills could reduce Marcia's mountain of evidence to dust. I had seen it happen in my own courtroom.

Peter rose and began to question Dr. Cotton in his thick Brooklyn accent. (Judge Ito would later complain that the court reporter had a hard time understanding Barry and Peter. He didn't seem too pleased to have the New Yorkers in his courtroom.)

Peter suggested to Cotton that blood at the crime scene may have been contaminated or tampered with. Contamination was becoming a central theme in the defense case, due to the unimpressive testimony of Dennis Fung, the chief criminalist at the scene. In a grueling nine days on the stand, Fung admitted making several errors in the collection process, including storing swatches with bloodstains in plastic bags.

But Peter wanted to cover all bases. He also challenged Cellmark's statistical calculations on the grounds that its database was not representative. The lab's database of African Americans was obtained from the Detroit Red Cross and consisted of DNA taken from only 240 people. Peter wanted to know how Cotton could get numbers in the billions from such a database.

Cotton disclosed that some data used for comparisons in the Simpson case included tests on only two other African Americans. She explained that in calculating the rarity of Simpson's genetic profile, she relied on five genetic markers.

"And so in your database, the number of people that you have typed like Mr. Simpson . . . is just two people, isn't that right?" Peter asked.

"Yes," Cotton said.

Although the sample of only two African Americans who were tested for all of the same genetic markers as Simpson was very small, Cotton said, "I don't think that's a critical feature." Even so, to a lay jury who did not fully understand the method of statistical calculations, the idea that only two African Americans were in the pool might raise significant doubt.

This was an area where the defense's clear mission was to confuse the jury. I tended to agree with Dr. Cotton that it meant very little, because, in truth, genetic testing transcends subgroups.

Peter moved on to the subject of contamination. He asked Dr. Cotton if the police criminalists in the case had improperly collected the evidence, thereby tainting the DNA. He pressed the idea that moisture and heat had degraded the DNA in such a way as to give faulty readings.

"Objection!" Woody was on his feet. "Dr. Cotton cannot testify to what she didn't see."

"Sustained," Ito said softly from the bench. "Ask another question."

Peter didn't miss a beat. "Isn't it true, Dr. Cotton, that putting wet bloodstains in plastic bags and leaving swatches in a locked truck without air-conditioning would not be your choice of procedures?"

"It wouldn't be my choice," Cotton agreed. "But real harm would only be caused if they were left that way for an extended period."

Peter turned a page on his notes and hunched over the lectern. "Let's turn to the blood found on the steering wheel of the Ford Bronco. Can you elaborate on what you found there?"

Cotton explained that the blood was a mixture of two people's DNA. Simpson and his former wife were a possible source, but one genetic marker in the blood was from an unknown source.

Peter raised his eyebrows and shot a meaningful look at the jury. "Could someone have touched Simpson's blood, touched Nicole Simpson's blood, and then touched the steering wheel?" he asked.

"Objection!" Woody shouted. "No foundation." This was clearly speculation on Peter's part.[*]

"Sustained," Ito said with a withering look to Neufeld.

Peter then turned to the credibility of the testing lab. Cotton conceded that in 1988 and 1989, her laboratory had twice made false matches in DNA testing due to sample-handling error or cross-contamination, in which blood from one sample was inadvertently mixed with blood from another. She noted, however, that the errors happened during quality-control tests, not actual DNA cases, and said Cellmark had undergone more than one hundred quality-control tests without mishaps since then.

But Peter wouldn't let her off the hook. An error was an error, whether it was in an actual case or a quality-control test. He suggested the lack of supervision for procedures at Cellmark cast doubt on the trustworthiness of its results, but Cotton held firm.

"Would you agree that you really have no scientific basis for estimating your laboratory's error rate?" Peter pressed.

Dr. Cotton was getting edgy. "No, I don't agree with that," she replied.

The two professionals continued to spar back and forth in this vein until Ito had finally had enough. "Wait!" he

---

[*]"Foundation" must be established before a question can legitimately be asked in a court of law. That is, lawyers are not allowed (although they are fond of breaking this rule) to ask anything that comes to mind. There must be a basis in the evidence to justify questions. Of course, this rule was broken rampantly in the Simpson case. I know that many lawyers figure the worst thing that can happen is the judge will sustain an objection. But even so, the question is out there. As lawyers like to say, "You can't unring a bell."

said sharply, holding up a hand. "Mr. Neufeld. Dr. Cotton. Stop arguing with each other and talking at the same time."

Dr. Cotton slumped in her chair, looking chastised. Peter smiled tightly. "Thank you, Your Honor. No more questions."

That night, the media buzzed with the news of how Peter had stood up to Dr. Cotton. In the careful hands of the prosecution, she'd seemed invincible, but when the ball was in his court, Peter had run with it. Such sports metaphors pervaded the nightly commentary during the Simpson trial. It had become, for better or worse, America's favorite pastime.

The following day, Woody Clark tried to put the prosecution back on track by calling a second witness to the stand to introduce scientific evidence linking O.J. Simpson to the murder of Ronald Goldman.

Gary Sims, a senior criminalist with the Department of Justice's DNA laboratory, told jurors that the blood taken from the glove found at Simpson's estate matched Goldman's blood.

Sims also supported Cotton's testimony that DNA tests of blood on the socks found in Simpson's bedroom matched Nicole's blood. About twenty stains were found on each sock.

But Sims's most meaningful moment came when he announced that blood consistent with Simpson's and the two victims was found inside the Bronco. It was the first time the jury had heard evidence of all three parties' blood being in the same location. It was highly incriminating.

In a dry voice whose clinical manner belied the impact of his words, Sims told the jury, "Three stains lifted from the center console of the vehicle appeared to be mixtures of blood containing the genetic patterns of Simpson, Nicole Brown Simpson, and Ronald Goldman. Another stain on the center console has the genetic material of Simpson and Goldman, and a stain on the driver-side carpet shows Nicole Simpson's genetic pattern. Two other stains only have Simpson's genetic signature."

There was a hush in the courtroom as Sims's voice droned on. It was the first time anyone had suggested that Goldman's blood was in Simpson's Ford Bronco.

"Mr. Sims, let's move on to the glove found at Mr. Simpson's Rockingham estate," Woody said. "Have you tested bloodstains found on that glove?"

"Yes," Sims nodded.

"Tell the jury what you found."

According to Sims, the blood of Simpson and the two victims was all over the glove, with most stains being a mixture.

Sims also offered important testimony about the location of the blood found on socks recovered from Simpson's bedroom. He testified that blood consistent with Nicole's was found near the ankle area, and that blood consistent with Simpson's was found in the toe area. The chances that the blood came from someone other than Nicole soared to an astronomical level—the combined calculations being one out of 21 billion, Sims said.

On cross-examination, Barry was determined to show that no matter how dramatic the statistics, none of it mattered if the blood was contaminated. After he had established the extremely sensitive nature of DNA testing, Barry asked Sims about the sloppy work habits of the Los Angeles police, including the use of unclean gloves and unsanitized tools. Might not these flaws have made a difference? he wondered. Failing to generate evidence of contamination, Barry would move to his next line of defense—police corruption.

"Do you know from your own personal knowledge how and when that blood got on the sock?" Barry asked, the aura of police misconduct hanging in the air.

Sims said no. He wouldn't, of course, since he hadn't been there, but the idea was out there in front of the jury.

Barry also harped on why the blood on the socks had not been visible to investigators. The suggestion was that the blood was planted later, in an attempt to frame Simpson.

Rock Harmon had a comeback for that. During his redirect examination of Sims, he asked that the jurors be allowed to step out of the jury box and one by one look through a crime-lab microscope at a "reddish" substance on one of the socks found in Simpson's home. Rock wanted them to see for themselves why no criminalist initially saw blood on either of the socks: the stains were not visible to the naked eye and only could be seen with the use of a microscope.

The jurors seemed glad to get up from their seats and move around. The DNA testimony had been numbing. But Rock couldn't tell if he'd made the point.

Well into the second week of DNA testimony, Rock Harmon faced Renee Montgomery, a criminalist with the state Department of Justice DNA lab, the third and final testing facility the prosecution employed. Rock was glad they'd decided to use three labs; surely the concurrence of all three about the DNA in this case proved the validity of the science. On the stand, Montgomery itemized the results of the DOJ lab:

- Three drops of blood in a trail leading away from the victims and three stains found on an iron gate outside Nicole's town house could all have been deposited by Simpson.
- Nicole and Ron could not have contributed to those blood drops.
- The bloodstains from the Bronco showed a mixture that contained the DNA patterns of Simpson, Nicole, and Ron.
- Stains on the bloody glove found behind Simpson's home also contained the DNA patterns of all three, with Ron appearing to be the main contributor of the blood.
- The DNA in the blood found on a pair of socks in Simpson's bedroom was consistent with Nicole's DNA pattern.

Marcia sat quietly at the prosecution table as the results of massive evidence, tested by three separate laboratories, made its way onto the large display boards perched in front of the jury. Occasionally, she glanced at the jurors' faces, hoping to detect a clue about their reaction. But they were inscrutable. She couldn't tell if the science of DNA was sinking in.

* * *

As the evidence continued to mount, Simpson's defense team turned up the heat, pressing the question of contamination. When Barry Scheck cross-examined police criminalist Collin Yamauchi, he focused on the defense theme that sloppy police and laboratory work contaminated the key evidence in the case. If they couldn't demonstrate major flaws in the DNA testing, they'd go to the source—the criminalists who collected and handled the specimens in the LAPD lab. Thus began what the defense would call the "garbage in, garbage out" portion of the case.

Barry spent an entire day pecking away at numerous areas of perceived weakness in the handling of evidence, as the jury looked on in bleary-eyed exhaustion. He tried to show that Yamauchi did not change gloves before handling different pieces of evidence, failed to adequately document blood testing, and generally did not follow rules designed to safeguard against contaminating the blood.

Shy and soft-spoken, with a nervous stutter, Yamauchi seemed a poor match for Barry's confident bulldog interrogation. He stumbled over his answers, and his demeanor on the stand made him *look* incompetent, even if he wasn't.

After four hours of battering away at Yamauchi, Barry hit pay dirt when Yamauchi said he suddenly remembered he got blood on his plastic gloves while handling a vial holding Simpson's blood sample.

"Aha!" Barry shouted with glee. "Mr. Yamauchi, is it possible that you could have transferred blood from your glove to other evidence?"

Yamauchi looked stunned. "No . . . I mean . . ."

"It's possible, isn't it?" Barry taunted him.

"Possible." He nodded slowly.

It was a point that would linger in the minds of the jury and be brought up repeatedly by the defense.

I wasn't at all surprised that Barry Scheck and Peter Neufeld were using contamination as their first line of defense. Contamination is a wonderful defense ploy to distract jurors from the evidence. People don't like to hear that evidence is contaminated. It's a word that suggests an odorous event. How can the evidence be valid if it's "contaminated"?

The problem is that it's false logic—although we can't really expect jurors who are not versed in the complexities of DNA to realize that. With DNA evidence, contamination will *exclude* a suspect, not *include* him. Contamination doesn't turn someone else's blood into *your* blood. In that respect, there's no difference between DNA and fingerprinting. If you've got a smudged fingerprint, you can't identify it as anyone's fingerprint. That's the case with DNA.

There is only one way to contaminate blood and thereby falsely include you: someone in the laboratory would have to deliberately take the contaminated DNA found at the scene, split it in half, and label one of the two resulting samples as your blood. No contamination can create a match—only human malevolence can.

In spite of everything Simpson's team suggested about problems in laboratories, what they didn't say was that out of hundreds of cases, there was no case on record that had ever demonstrated the existence of a false positive.

Of course, creating a morass of confusion and doubt was exactly what the defense team had in mind. It was their job, and I didn't fault them for it, but it still troubled me. I knew that if you go into a courtroom and use scientific language and concepts that are hard to understand, and then throw in the possibility of contamination, you're going to cause great distraction and doubt in the jury.

I found it meaningful that very little argument arose about the manner in which the tests were performed; that was refreshing. But lacking questions about the testing, the defense was forced to go back and raise questions about planting of blood evidence and prior contamination. This strategy seemed spurious to anyone who truly understood the science. But perhaps not to the jury, for whom all of this material was new.

The defense team was expertly sowing, bit by bit, the seeds of reasonable doubt. Barry and Peter knew that all it took was nagging questions that could not be answered, and the creation of such nagging questions could be accomplished in virtually every case. Indeed, the presence of so much evidence aided the defense in this respect.

On July 24, Peter called Fredric Reiders, a forensic toxicologist and founder of the National Medical Services Laboratory, in Willow Grove, Pennsylvania, to the stand. He was the first witness they used in their effort to show that Simpson was a victim of a police conspiracy.

Reiders testified that blood found on a sock in Simpson's bedroom and on a back gate of Nicole's home contained a substance known as EDTA. EDTA is a chemical preservative placed in tubes to prevent collected blood from clotting. It is also naturally present in small amounts in all blood, as well as in certain chemical detergents.

The defense claimed that the presence of EDTA on the sock proved the blood came, not during a struggle, but from a vial of Nicole's autopsy blood; and the blood on the gate came from a vial of blood Simpson gave to police the day after the murders.

Reiders testified that even though EDTA is present in human blood, its presence is minimal. The quantity of EDTA in the two bloodstains, he said, was much higher. He speculated that if a person had that much EDTA in his blood, there would be no clotting and he'd be dead.

The evidence about the presence of EDTA hurt the prosecution. Again, it was so complex that one could hardly expect a jury to comprehend it. Marcia feared they would be left with an impression, if not a "clear" understanding, that the presence of EDTA indicated that evidence had been tampered with. She knew that she would have to discredit Reiders in some way. The only thing she had going for her was Judge Ito's ruling that she could question Reiders on mistakes he'd allegedly made in a past murder case.

When it was her turn to cross-examine Reiders, Marcia went after him aggressively.

Hour after hour, she slammed into Reiders about an alleged mistake in the case of a funeral-home director accused in the death of a competitor. Reiders had concluded the victim could have died of oleander poisoning, but subsequent tests found no sign of oleander, and charges against the defendant were dismissed.

Marcia also tried to show that Reiders had misread an Environmental Protection Agency report, and that humans actually had much more EDTA in their blood than he said.

She was tired when she finally sat down, and a bit discouraged. Had any of it made a bit of sense to the jury?

The next day, the prosecution had another chance to discredit the defense's theory about EDTA. Roger Martz, the FBI scientist who had originally conducted the tests, stated firmly that Reiders had misread the results. In fact, Martz announced, he had tested his own unpreserved blood and found the same amount of EDTA that was on the sock and the gate. "Fredric Reiders jumped to conclusions," he asserted. There was no way that the data showed high levels of EDTA on the two pieces of evidence.

Marcia was pleased with Martz's testimony, but in the battle of the experts, she couldn't say which view had prevailed.

Watching Marcia try to convince the jury that no evidence was planted, I knew what a struggle it was. Often in a case, the merest suggestion, the slightest hint of misconduct, is enough to cause the jury simply to disregard *all* of the evidence.

But if you really examined it logically, step-by-step, you would have to question *how* a conspiracy was possible. If the defense proposed that the police planted evidence, didn't they have an obligation to show how this might have been done? The defense took great joy in presenting testimony that Mark Fuhrman, a detective on the scene, was a racist, and that was enough to assume that he might have, and probably did, try to frame Simpson by planting the glove at Rockingham. But that was still a very long way from proving, by means of actual evidence, that he had motive or opportunity to plant evidence in this case. It was a longer way still from showing how virtually every piece of evidence—even those Fuhrman never touched—was planted.

Was the mere suggestion of impropriety enough? I believe this points to a problem in the procedures of the criminal justice system. We talk about a trial being a search for the truth, but we don't always get closer to the truth. We allow attorneys to stray from it. To dance around it. To distort it. They tell the jury to look to the right, to look to the left, to look up, to look down, to look everywhere except straight ahead to where the truth is.

So, the defense team suggested that someone planted the blood. But they never answered the question of who had an opportunity to do it. And not just one drop, but all of the many pieces of evidence. There was DNA everywhere, not just one drop of it.

The defense proposed that the indisputable fact that the DNA belonged to Simpson lost its strength and value because of the EDTA. That was a nonissue, in my opinion. But how on earth could you expect a jury to understand EDTA? And that's exactly *why* the defense used it in their strategy. The system permits that. It permits confusion to rear its ugly head in the jury—as a tool for the defense.

I believe that the matter of EDTA should have been

resolved by an independent expert appointed by the court to determine the issue and then present the result, so the information would have been clear to the jury. Instead, it was a free-for-all of experts disputing one another. In the end, this obfuscation favored the defense, because all it did was plant doubt: *I don't understand, therefore I have doubt.*

The next day, in a hearing without the presence of the jury, Judge Ito listened to the defense argue that they be allowed to bring in further testimony to the LAPD crime lab's sloppiness.

"This is the heart of our defense," Barry argued. "The key defense contention regarding DNA is that because of substandard practices in this county, key evidence was cross-contaminated. This has been our contention since opening statements."

Marcia fought vigorously against the motion. "You see what they're trying to do," she told Ito. "They're trying to mislead and confuse the jury. Don't let that happen, Your Honor."

Judge Ito said he would allow the testimony out of fairness because the prosecution was given great latitude in presenting its elaborate DNA evidence. "The PCR-based DNA testing is sophisticated and subject to problems like contamination," he said. Therefore, defense expert Dr. John Gerdes could testify about problems with PCR and widespread contamination within the LA crime lab.

Dr. John Gerdes, the clinical director at Immunological Associates in Denver, had studied the competence of twenty-three forensic cases in cities across the United

States. He said the work of the prosecution's DNA experts was, at best, unreliable.

"The LAPD crime lab is a cesspool of contamination," Gerdes told the jury. "It is chronic in the sense that it doesn't go away."

Barry presented a chart showing a list of problems in forensic testing that create a higher risk of contamination and error. These include dirty samples, minuscule sample sizes, mixed samples from unknown sources, multiple handling, and statistical controversy.

But under cross-examination, Dr. Gerdes admitted that he had never conducted a forensic experiment and could not categorically deny that O.J. Simpson and Ronald Goldman were the source of the blood found in Simpson's Ford Bronco.

The defense was doing an expert job of chipping away at the prosecution's mountain of DNA evidence. But Rock Harmon had another ace in his hand.

"Your Honor," he said before the trial resumed the following morning, "we have in our possession the results of a final RFLP test, just completed. It shows that blood found under the console of Simpson's Ford Bronco matches Simpson and Ron Goldman."

Ito was annoyed. "Why is this test just coming in now?"

Rock shrugged. "RFLP takes time, Your Honor. This is a critical piece of evidence. I submit to you that it is the 'other shoe' in our DNA case."

Ito reluctantly agreed that the state could present the evidence during its rebuttal. It turned out to have less impact than Rock thought. By then, the jury was clearly tired of hearing about DNA. It may have seemed to them that the prosecution was overdoing it. What did it matter if there was *more* DNA if, as the defense suggested, it either originated in a cesspool of contamination or had been planted?

Finally, the man who was perhaps the defense's most important witness, Dr. Henry Lee, rose to testify, and he made an unforgettable impression on the jury.

"Something is wrong here," he said in his heavily accented voice. "I look at the crime scene and I look at the evidence, and I think something is wrong."

Lee was a master on the stand—charming and persuasive. He knew how to talk to a jury in terms they could understand, and he painted the most vivid image of the trial as he spoke of contamination.

"It's like eating a plate of spaghetti. Looking through the bowl, you see a cockroach. Do you then take every strand in the bowl of spaghetti and look for more cockroaches? No"—he smiled—"you just throw it away."

Several jurors smiled. At the defense table, Simpson beamed at Lee. Across the aisle, Marcia stared stonily ahead. How ironic that a forensic expert who normally testified on behalf of the prosecution would be the one to maneuver the jury closer to an acquittal.

As Judge Ito prepared to instruct the jury, I empathized with the difficulty of his task. I remembered well how overwhelmed I felt during the *Castro* hearing, before I had a full understanding of the science of DNA testing. It seemed grossly unfair that our system would simply toss a judge into a setting where he is forced to act as an expert on such technical and complex material. As I have done many times in the past, I wondered why our system does not permit a judge to have an expert witness of his own. Why shouldn't a judge be able to call on someone and say, "Listen, I have a case dealing with DNA. I want you to teach me what this is all about"?

There's no provision for that, however. And to my knowledge, no one has ever suggested it. It's yet another issue we haven't bothered to tackle, and frankly, it's irritating to the people who love this system. It shows a lack of accountability, of caring, of aggressiveness, of willingness to learn. But those of us who want to do the right thing suffer because of the way the system is shaped.

That's my pet peeve. And I was aware that it was this very problem that would cause Judge Ito to stumble again and again. Not because he wasn't an intelligent man or a good judge—but because he wasn't allowed the independent resources that would have enabled him to judge most wisely. In our system, a judge is forced to learn right along with the jury.

On September 28, nearly nine months into the trial, Barry Scheck rose in the hushed courtroom and approached the jury box. The lead defense attorney, Johnnie Cochran, had selected him to give the all-important closing arguments on DNA. Cochran himself had already spoken—painting the defense's case in broader, more emotional tones. With the fiery passion of an evangelist, Cochran decried police corruption, racism, deceit. His words brought tears to the eyes of several in the mostly African American jury. He painted Detective Mark

Fuhrman as a "genocidal racist," comparing him to Adolf Hitler. He urged the jury to "send a message" that they would not tolerate police corruption. It was a performance worthy of a cathedral, if not a court of law. Now Barry would do the DNA mop-up—showing the jury that they could not believe the evidence. As he began speaking, his voice was uncharacteristically soft.

"The integrity of this system is at stake. You cannot convict when the core of the prosecution's case is built on perjurious testimony of police officers, unreliable forensic evidence, and manufactured evidence," he said. "There are many, many reasonable doubts buried right in the heart of the scientific evidence in this case, and we have demonstrated them. And we don't have to prove them, but the evidence shows it.

"So, in the words of Dr. Lee, something is wrong. Something is terribly wrong with the evidence in this case. You cannot trust it; it lacks integrity. It cannot be a basis for a verdict beyond a reasonable doubt."

Barry sauntered closer to the jury, and raised his voice several notches.

"Ms. Clark told you in the opening statement that collecting and preserving bloodstain evidence for purposes of DNA testing was as simple as going into your kitchen and cleaning up spillage. Now, we all know that's not true, based on what we have heard in this case.

"Let's start with the sock. We know that on June thirteenth when Mr. Fung went to collect the sock, he saw it on the throw rug . . . and he did not see blood. He did not see soil on the carpet. He did not see any trace evidence around, not on the stairwell, not on the carpet, leading into the bedroom, not anywhere.

"There's supposedly a stain, an ankle stain on these socks—you saw it cut out—about an inch and a half, more DNA in that than anything in this case. Wouldn't that, if it were there, have left a transfer, some specks, something, if they were in a struggle?"

He appealed to the jury's reason and experience. "You have children. I have children. Do you ever see them go out to play in dirt like that closed-in area at Bundy, get into some kind of ruckus, socks come back, they are filthy? It would have to be here if there is anything on them at all. Nothing. Nothing there."

Barry paused for effect and stared down at his notes for a moment before continuing.

"In your deliberations, somebody may say, 'All right, I have a reasonable doubt about this essential piece of evidence, the socks . . . that they manufactured this piece of evidence, but let's put that aside and look at everything else.'

"Well, just wait a second. Just think about what that means. If they manufactured evidence on the sock, how can you trust anything else? How, in this country, in this democracy, can they come in—there is no doubt Fuhrman's a liar and a genocidal racist, there is no doubt about that, but there is really no doubt, either, that they played with this sock. Is there? And if that can happen, that is a reasonable doubt for this case."

Barry now began to pick up speed, and his voice grew sharper as he questioned each piece of evidence. "In terms of assessing hair and fiber evidence, you have to look at the issue of contamination," he told the jury. "Particularly when you are talking about hair and fiber flying all over the place at a crime scene. I mean, this is where the issue of contaminating a scene is of critical importance, and how did they handle this scene? There were twenty-three stains tested. Sixteen of those stains showed carryover. And very interestingly, if Mr. Simpson supposedly committed these murders and his hand was cut and he was struggling here, no matches. No evidence of his blood on this clothing. But there is carry-over between the clothing.

"Now, what does that mean? That means, frankly, that the bodies were dragged through the crime scene and blood from Nicole Brown Simpson got on Mr. Goldman and vice versa, and if that happens, that's how the fibers can get carried over, too. And Ms. Clark went on and on with this rank speculation where she was saying it was one killer, and we know it was one killer because we saw some fibers that came from Nicole's dress and got on Ron's shirt or jeans and got back and forth, and that's how we know one person was going back and forth between the victims.

"Nonsense. This proves it. This proves that the hair and fiber and the blood evidence were all coming together because the handling of this crime scene is a disgrace, a disgrace. They are dragging the bodies back and forth."

Barry went on for long minutes, waving his hands dramatically, building a word picture of a horrible mess. Finally, he ended: "It is a cancer at the heart of this case, and that's what this evidence shows when you go through it patiently, when you go through it carefully, when you go through it scientifically, logically. That's what the evidence shows."

Barry sat down, and Judge Ito called a recess. The drama in the courtroom was reaching a climax. Now the prosecution would have a final chance to make its case to the jury.

As Marcia rose from her seat, she turned to look at the families of the victims. In the center of the courtroom, Ron Goldman's father and sister huddled together, as they had throughout the trial, not trying to mask the tears that coursed down their cheeks. Beside them sat Nicole's mother and her two sisters, slumped in their seats with the weight of their emotional exhaustion. Marcia had never lost sight of her obligation to these family members whose pain was unimaginable. Now her voice shook with weariness and rage.

"I don't know how much clearer it could be. I really don't," she said. "Once you see the vast array of physical evidence, you can see that there is virtually an ocean of evidence to prove that this defendant committed these murders. What all of this evidence does, it links the defendant to the victims and the crime scene at Bundy. . . .

"His blood on the rear gate with that match makes him one in fifty-seven billion people that could have left that blood. I mean, there are only five billion people on the planet . . . that is an identification that proves it is his blood; nobody else's on the planet. No one.

"Now, Nicole's blood on the socks, I believe to be one in six-point-eight billion people. Again, her blood and only hers on this planet could be on that sock. The blood on the Bundy trail comes back to the defendant because it is his blood. The blood on the rear gate comes back to the defendant because it is blood he left there on the night of the murders."

Marcia blew out her breath. Her eyes were flashing as she made her final impassioned plea to the jury, begging them not to be tricked by innuendos the defense could not prove. Her face was very pale, almost bloodless looking, but her voice was strong.

"I want to hear Mr. Cochran actually stand up in front of you and tell you he believes the blood was planted," she raged. "I want to hear that because that is incredible, absolutely incredible.

"The defense has thrown out many, many other questions. They've thrown out questions about whether LAPD has some bad police officers; does the scientific division have some sloppy criminalists; does the coroner's office have some sloppy coroners. And the answer to all these questions is sure, yes, they do. That's not news to you. I'm sure it wasn't a big surprise to you.

"They're important issues. You know, we should look into the quality control. Things should be done better. Things could always be done better in every case, at every time. There's no question about that. We're not here to vote on that today."

Finally, her voice softening, Marcia returned to what she believed was the heart of the matter—the tortured relationship between Simpson and Nicole that she contended set a motive for murder. She played a tape of one of Nicole's emergency 911 calls, in 1993, in which she pleaded for police help: "He's back. He's O.J. Simpson. I think you know his record." As the tape was played, images from Nicole's life were flashed for jurors: her battered face; a picture of her at a police station; her pants dirty from a fall in the mud; a swollen arm.

The screen then showed a series of photos taken in 1994: black socks at the foot of Simpson's bed; the bloody glove at his Rockingham estate; the blood drops on Simpson's driveway; Simpson's Ford Bronco; blood on the Bundy Drive walkway.

And then, finally, the screen filled with the tightest shot yet of Nicole Simpson's body lying at the foot of the steps outside her home. It was followed by a close-up of Ron Goldman's crumpled body in a gated area.

Marcia's voice dropped to barely above a whisper. "I don't have to say anything else," she said. "Ladies and gentlemen, on behalf of the people of the state of California, because we have proven beyond a reasonable doubt, far beyond a reasonable doubt, that the defendant committed these murders, we ask you to find the defendant guilty of murder in the first degree of Ronald Goldman and Nicole Brown Simpson."

At last, it was the jury's turn. And no one could know how they would perceive the evidence once they were behind closed doors. Marcia had asked them to look at a mountain of DNA evidence. The defense had urged them to focus on the doubts and inconsistencies. But would these lead to what the jurors could conceive of as a reasonable doubt?

Reasonable doubt is the high standard that exists in a criminal justice system. But what is it? That's a very relevant question, especially when you're talking about DNA. If a juror thinks to himself, "I don't really understand all of this scientific stuff, so I have a doubt about it," does that mean he has reasonable doubt as defined in a court of law? Certainly, that's what the defense would hope.

Ultimately, the jurors can only use their common sense, and apply their own knowledge to the reliability of the evidence: Was there blood where it shouldn't have been? Were there footprints where there shouldn't have been? Was there a bloody glove where it shouldn't have been? Was there a cut on the hand that was not explained? These might all be clues that pointed to guilt.

But these were not easily answered questions, so the defense rushed in to fill the void with doubt. He cut his hand on a glass in Chicago. Those aren't his shoes. The glove didn't fit. There is no knife. The blood was planted. (Or, if it wasn't planted, it was contaminated.)

Reasonable doubt does not mean *any* doubt. DNA is usually present in conjunction with other evidence, and these are important, too. Anything is possible, but what is reasonable? How many people had a motive? How many people knew where Nicole lived? How many people had blood in their cars? How many people left blood at the scene? And so on. These are the factors that a jury could use to establish guilt. It's certainly not enough to say, "I have doubt about one piece of evidence, so that taints the whole case."

Deciding reasonable doubt is really very similar to the way people make other decisions in their lives. Suppose, for example, you have a severe leg injury. One doctor says you have to have your right leg removed. You want a second opinion. Why? Because you have questions. You have doubt that this is the right choice. Now, the second doctor says the leg can be saved. Now you have two opinions and they conflict.

What do you do? You probably seek even more opinions, weigh the credentials of all the experts, and read everything you can get your hands on. But in the end, you may still find yourself with some conflicting recommendations. Ultimately, you'll have to use your judgment, common sense, and life experience to decide what to do.

This is life. Here is another example. Suppose you live in New York and a good job opens up across the country in California. You're settled right now, with a family, a terrific job, a comfortable home. The new job has interesting potential and pays more money, but it's in California. Should you take it?

What information would you look for? What's the climate? What's the real-estate situation? What security would you have? That's the kind of important judgment you would use. Could you be positive? No. Are you absolutely guaranteed your decision will be correct? No.

In the Simpson case, if all you had was a coincidence involving a cut on the defendant's hand, that would certainly allow reasonable doubt. But when you combine the alleged coincidences with things that are not coincidences, like the presence of the victims' blood in the Bronco, and the trails of blood leading from the vehicle to his house, and the presence of Nicole's blood on his socks found in his bedroom, how could you explain it?

Do you have absolute proof? Well, no one saw him do it. But are you comfortable about concluding that all of the evidence points overwhelmingly to his guilt?

Was it reasonable to believe that police planted evidence to frame Simpson for this crime? That they wanted to blame Simpson and let the real killer of two people go free? Was it reasonable to believe that they wanted Simpson charged with a crime he didn't commit, in a state that carries a death penalty? Why? Because he was married to a white woman? Was that reasonable?

The jury must decide. And what many people do not know is that juries have a secret weapon called nullification. That is, they may, by law, simply choose to disregard all of the evidence and go with their gut feelings, or their biases, or their hidden agendas, or their false assumptions. There is no mandate that forces rigorous scrutiny in the jury room.

Marcia Clark knew that as she watched the jurors file out of the courtroom. It was in their hands now, and there was finally nothing more that could be said.

CHAPTER 9

The Verdict

In the valley of the blind, the one-eyed man is king.

—ERASMUS

"We, the jury, in the above-entitled action, find the defendant, Orenthal James Simpson, not guilty of the crime of murder. . . ."

In the room where we were listening to the verdict, there was a rush of air as twenty court officers, secretaries, and lawyers let out their breath in simultaneous awe. Simpson was free.

My law secretary, Julia, turned to me with wide eyes. She was plainly shocked, but to tell you the truth, I wasn't. It was unlikely that a jury would deliberate for less than four hours and then send a man to prison for life. Frankly, no matter what the verdict, I was appalled that after all the months of testimony, the jury seemingly had not bothered to deliberate at all. I had many unanswered questions, and the biggest one, of course, was the jury's take on DNA. I hoped it wasn't true, as one headline proposed, that DNA IS DOA. At the same time, there was no way I could conceive that a jury could really examine the DNA evidence in such a short period of time. My guess was they'd bought the corruption/contamination argument of the defense. But what did that mean for DNA?

In the days and weeks to come, one thing became clear: no matter what anyone said, the Simpson case could not be a valid test for forensic DNA because the jurors had simply ignored it altogether. They never studied the evidence. They didn't debate it. They didn't turn their deliberations into an intelligent scrutiny worthy of the many months of testimony that had preceded them.

It struck me strongly as I listened to the jurors who spoke after the trial that it's probably not fair to expect average people to learn this or other similarly dense scientific material, especially when the scientists themselves are in disagreement about its validity. How could you possibly expect juries to comprehend complexities that judges and lawyers have difficulty understanding? I had suspected, frankly, that there was going to be a problem in the Simpson case when the autorad was handed to Judge Ito and he looked at it upside down. Nobody bothered to inform him that he was holding it the wrong way. I didn't blame him for this because I remember, back in *Castro*, I had the same difficulty. It's a failure of the system that allows that gap in judicial knowledge.

The presentation of DNA evidence in the Simpson case was one of the best I've ever seen. However, that mattered little if the judge was not well versed in the science and could not control the proceedings. The key has to be the judge. He can't take a backseat while lawyers are busy complicating the process and obfuscating the truth.

Many people have said that the verdict in the Simpson case has discredited DNA; that it was a vote against such testing as a truth-seeking tool. But if you look at it clearly, you can't really say that the jurors discounted the DNA. What the jurors said was that apparently the glove and socks were planted, and if the glove and socks were planted, the DNA was irrelevant. The trouble is that the jurors' thinking was limited and superficial. They didn't analyze the evidence, they didn't think logically, and they managed not to be impressed with the strong, unassailable truth of the facts.

There was no deliberation in this case. And when you don't deliberate, you don't deliberate for a reason— because your mind is made up. This makes you a poor judge of the evidence, but as I've said, nullification— the decision to ignore evidence—is within the power of the jury.

Of course, the jurors have denied that it was a case of jury nullification. Several of them explained the brief deliberation by saying, "We did deliberate. We did nothing *but* deliberate for nine long months!" There's no other way to interpret such a statement than to assume that at least some of the jurors ignored the judge's instructions and formed opinions prior to the end of the trial. That bothered me. I suspect it is not an isolated case.

I think the Simpson case said more about the jury system than it did about the validity of forensic DNA. What's the magic in allowing twelve people, inexperienced in the law, inexperienced in analyzing complicated evidence, to determine the truth? As radical as it sounds, we could even allow the judge to go into the jury room with the jury and participate in the process. It's done in many democratic systems throughout the world, but we persist in believing in the magic of the jury as we've established it.

What do you do about juries who don't have the education and, therefore, the ability to evaluate complicated scientific evidence? It's up to the lawyers to pick or not pick particular people. But they have hidden agendas. Their agenda is to pick a juror who's going to save their client or convict the accused. And in that respect, the system is flawed.

I must admit that I am disappointed in the result in the Simpson case. It affects the issue of DNA testing because now everyone expects such test results to be introduced during a trial. If you can't introduce them, you're going to get an acquittal. If you do introduce them, everyone remembers the Simpson shambles and becomes skeptical about their validity. The bizarre procedures in California have affected the whole system.

It's a problem with the adversarial system, as opposed to an inquisitorial system, such as the one practiced in France. There, the magistrate investigating the crime orders a DNA test. The test is performed, it's shown to the lawyers, and it comes into evidence. There is no dispute about it. Perhaps it is time we take a second look at other judicial systems to determine if we can improve our own.

So, the question remains: what is the future of forensic DNA evidence in the courtrooms of America?

I have no question about the validity of DNA forensic evidence. But we learned a hard lesson in the *Castro* case. It matters that the scientific tests are performed properly. If they are, there is virtually no danger that an innocent person will be wrongfully convicted.

If the tests are performed correctly, there will be one

of three results: an accurate result, an inconclusive result, or no result at all. An innocent person cannot be in jeopardy from a DNA test unless the technician is downright malevolent. But that is true for any forensic science. With DNA, contamination, sloppy lab work, or poor analysis is easily detected by the experts and the result is to give a guilty person an advantage—not to point the finger at an innocent person. We need not fear that DNA evidence will put innocent people in jail.

Indeed, in *People v. Lindsey Calhoun*, a rape case I recently decided, DNA tests showed conclusively that the DNA recovered from the sperm had not come from the defendant. I dismissed the indictment, and a falsely accused person went free.

Another problem is statistical analysis. As Erasmus said, "In the valley of the blind, the one-eyed man is king." That's the danger posed by DNA statisticians who sweep into the courtroom and dazzle us with numerical sleight of hand. The numbers generated do not speak the truth. The fear that DNA evidence is too powerful has reduced the use of this evidence to the point of absurdity. As use of the science has grown in the legal system, we have seen the figures go from the incomprehensible (such as one in 738 trillion) to the absurd (such as one in seventeen) for a four-probe match. We have dangerously strayed from our legal principles by allowing statisticians to invade our criminal justice system. It distresses me.

We must take back our system from the scientists. That may seem like harsh language coming from a judge who supports the introduction of DNA evidence in criminal trials. But here's the problem: since the statisticians use a different language than the one we're familiar with in law, judges and juries cannot properly evaluate the information they present.

In every other forensic science, we ask the clear and simple question of the scientist on the witness stand: "Can you state, with a reasonable degree of scientific certainty, if the unknown item came from the disputed sample?" The question has historically been the same whether the disputed sample is a fingerprint, bullet, hair, tooth, fiber, glass, or footprint. It's clearly understandable, and more important, it actually contributes to the effort to reach the truth. The issue of whether the defendant is connected in some way to a disputed sample gets raised and answered.

However, in forensic DNA evidence, this issue has become entwined with double-talk and irrelevancies that have no other purpose than to confuse and distract juries. For example, shouldn't we be concerned about the probability of the defendant having the same genetic patterns as a disputed sample—rather than the odds of *anyone else* having the same patterns? Shouldn't we be asking simply whether it's probable, likely, or whether the defendant is excluded altogether?

The meaning of statistics as applied to forensic DNA is the continuing problem that plagues this science. And until we address the issue, what is arguably the greatest advance in the criminal justice system in many decades will remain in boondoggle, subject to different interpretations by every jury that encounters it.

The message of DNA forensic evidence is strong and clear. It can dramatically point the finger at the guilty.

But just as important, it can swiftly and certainly exonerate the innocent. In the great scheme that forms our system of justice, we can agree that there is nothing more horrible than the conviction of an innocent person.

This is the magic of DNA. It can be used to avoid that horrible occurrence. In the end, when testing is properly performed, DNA forensic evidence is an invaluable aid in the search for truth—no matter on which end of the scale it may land.

I am well aware that even without the gymnastics that occurred in the Simpson courtroom, the jury might *still* have chosen to ignore the DNA evidence. In our system, juries have that power. I hope, however, that this stance will go the way of that old proclamation, held so long and so destructively despite overwhelming evidence to the contrary: "The world is flat."

Sadly, I'm not confident this will happen.

The day after the verdict in the case of O.J. Simpson, I returned to my own murder case to begin the grueling process of jury selection. The case involved a street murder, an argument over drug territory, the death of a young white man at the hands of a young black man.

I began questioning the panel of prospective jurors. I told them I appreciated their taking the time to do their civic duty, knowing that the majority of jury summonses that go out in our city are simply ignored.

As it is in most of my cases, the people in my jury pool were mostly African American and Hispanic. Did that mean there would be a racial verdict, that they would acquit the black man regardless of the evidence?

There are many who believe that the verdict in the Simpson case was racially motivated—that a majority African American jury was simply not going to send this man to prison. As I looked into the faces of my own mostly black jury pool, I recognized this as a problem.

There's no point in beating around the bush or trying to pretend it's otherwise. It's a simple fact that racially motivated verdicts are a reality. The conviction rate in Bronx County is about sixty percent, meaning that forty percent of the people who come to trial are acquitted. What does this statistic mean? That nearly half the people arrested in Bronx County are falsely arrested?

Of course not. The answer is simple: juries are often refusing to send more black youths to jail. It's the message they hear in the sermons preached Sundays in the black churches—to stop the madness of one in three black youths being in jail. And the message gets brought into the courtroom.

Sadly, those very people who acquit defendants for racial motivations refuse to recognize the great majority of people that live in the same area who are honest, law-abiding, unprejudiced, decent, hardworking, oppressed, poor—and don't commit crimes. They're the victims. The jurors themselves are more likely to be victims of crime than most Americans.

I can understand the anger in this community toward the police and the criminal justice system. Some of it may be warranted. But we must protect our system. So if juries are going to start deciding that they will ignore evidence, or play God with the evidence, or use their power to free people they know to be guilty, then maybe we should consider suspending the jury system and revert to a panel of judges. Not that this will ever happen. But it dismays me to think that the passions of a community are speaking through the judicial system.

There are solutions, but we're not able to get to them because people are not thinking straight about this problem.

It's not always racial verdicts that are troubling. In my most recent case, a DNA case, there were no racial overtones because the defendant and the victim were both African American, and the issue was strictly the truth of the testimony of the woman who said that her boyfriend raped her. Initially, the boyfriend said, "I never even touched her." But when the DNA test results indicated that it was his semen that had been found on the victim, he changed his story and said, "Yes, we had sex, but she consented."

This was one of the very few cases where the lawyers picked almost the first twelve jurors who were seated in the box. There were very few peremptory challenges. As it turned out, five people on the jury didn't believe in date rape. The case ended in a hung jury because those five people brought their personal biases into the case.

So I have to wonder, if juries have their own agendas—of race or gender or religion, or other biases—how on earth can we expect them to judge plain science? We can advance this science until kingdom come, establish committees and rules and procedures all we want. But will it really make much difference in the long run? This is the discouraging reality.

These are not abstract or theoretical musings. We are talking about flesh and blood.

In my apartment, I keep a scrapbook containing pictures from all of the murder cases that have been tried in my courtroom. Some people might find this disconcerting. For me, it's a constant reminder of the lives that rest in our hands. When I turn the pages of my scrapbook, I remind myself that these were vital lives once, people whose hearts pumped, whose minds were clear, humans who laughed and cried. In death, covered in the bloody shroud of violence, they are frozen in time as a testimony to the destructive impulses within our society.

I think of the words, "Blood will tell."

But will we listen?

APPENDIX A

Commonly Used Terms in Forensic DNA

adenine: One of the four bases found in the DNA helix; will only combine with thymine.

agarose gel: A gelatinlike substance into which DNA is loaded for electrophoresis.

allele: One specific form of a given gene.

anonymous loci: Specific sites on a chromosome where the gene functions have not been identified.

autorad: An X-ray film of the hybridization between the radioactive probe and the complementary exposed strand of DNA.

autoradiography: The process of making an autorad.

bacterial DNA: The DNA found in bacteria.

band: A radioactive signal on an autorad usually caused by a fragment of human or bacterial DNA that combines with a radio-labeled DNA probe.

band shifting: Bands that should comigrate, but don't. Band shifting is commonly caused by DNA degradation, but other causes might apply.

base pair: The combination of either adenine and thymine, or cytosine and guanine. Base pairs form the rungs of the DNA helix (spiral ladder).

bin or binning: A conservative method of calculating population frequency by combining groups of fragment sizes into defined groups instead of making calculations from a single fragment size.

blot: Same as Southern blot.

ceiling principle: A highly conservative method of calculating allele frequencies in populations by stating that any frequency below 10 percent must be reported as 10 percent. Its purpose is to eliminate bias based upon ethnic subgroups.

chromosomes: A discrete unit of the genome carrying many genes. Each human has forty-six chromosomes.

cocktail autorad: A single autorad showing two or more loci that have been hybridized at the same time.

complementary strand of DNA: A strand of DNA that binds to another because its base pairs are complementary; e.g., ATTACG, which will only combine with TAATGC.

complete digestion: The action of a restriction enzyme in completely cutting the DNA at a specific site.

confidence level: Degree of confidence expressed when two samples of DNA can be said to be the same or different.

contaminated DNA: DNA that contains bacterial, viral, or other nonhuman DNA.

contaminated probe: A DNA probe on which a small percentage of the cloning substance used in its manufacture is present.

control lane: An electrophoresis lane that contains a known sample of human DNA.

cross-hybridization: A piece of DNA; a probe manufactured to bind with a specific sequence of single-stranded DNA that binds with many DNAs because of sequence similarities or relaxed stringency conditions.

cytosine: One of the four bases found in the DNA helix; will only combine with guanine.

database: An empirically derived group of DNA types obtained by DNA typing people of known ethnicity.

degradation of DNA: The destruction of expected sequences of DNA by an outside source, chemical or otherwise.

denaturation: The process of unzipping the double helix and exposing a single strand of DNA; accomplished during the Southern blot procedure.

digitizer: A digitizing camera, digitizing mouse, or digitizing tablet that is used to measure the fragment sizes of bands on autorads.

dirty autorad: Background marks, contamination, or other items on an autorad other than DNA; also called "schmutz."

DNA: Deoxyribonucleic acid.

DNA diagnostics: The use of DNA to diagnose disease.

DNA fingerprinting, typing, identification, and forensics: The legal use of DNA testing as evidence in court.

double helix: The DNA molecule with two connected complementary strands of DNA.

DQ-Alpha: A gene located in the sixth chromosome used in PCR.

DXYS14, D2S44, D17S79, DYZ1, D10S28, D5S110, D1S7, and D4S139: Various loci involved with DNA RFLP forensic identification.

DYZ1: Locus on Y chromosome specific for males.

electrophoresis: Electric current applied to agarose gel permitting DNA bands to travel from the negative to the positive pole in the gel.

enzyme: A protein that catalyzes a biochemical reaction.

enzyme digestion: The action of the restriction enzyme in cutting the DNA.

ethidium bromide: Dye usually used to stain DNA.

exclusion: DNA banding patterns that do not match.

extraction and isolation of DNA: The process of removing and purifying DNA from the nucleus of a cell.

false positive, false exclusion, false inclusion, false negative, or false match: Erroneous reading of a human or nonhuman band of DNA on an autorad.

floating bins: A method of binning DNA fragment sizes where the bins float rather than being fixed. It is a conservative method of calculating allele frequencies from DNA databases.

fragment: A piece of DNA cut by a restriction enzyme; also known as a band on an autorad.

gender probes: Probes designed to determine the sex of DNA, be it male or female.

gene: Section of DNA, located within a chromosome, that is responsible for some function; e.g., gene for eye color.

genome: The total pool of genetic information of an organism found in the cell nucleus.

genotype: Combination of specific alleles found in an individual's DNA.

guanine: One of the four bases found in the DNA helix; will only combine with cytosine.

Human Gene Mapping Conference: Program to collect data on mapping the human genome.

hybridization: The process of combining radioactive probes with unzipped strands of DNA to allow for the connection of adenine to thymine and cytosine to guanine.

immunogenetics: Molecular genetics of the immune system.

inclusion: The visual and computer measurement of DNA fragments on an autorad. For multiple probe matches, these fragments are deemed indistinguishable and therefore are from the same person.

indistinguishable bands or fragments: Bands or fragments of DNA on an autorad that are calculated to be within a scientifically acceptable range to allow a declaration of a match.

karyotype: Analysis of 46 chromosomes in a person.

kilobase or "Kb" pairs: One thousand base pairs.

lane-loading with DNA: Filling wells on tip of gel with DNA prior to electrophoresis.

lane of gel: The path in the gel within which DNA fragments migrate.

lane smear: A dark staining in an elecrophoretic lane caused by degraded DNA.

loci: Plural of locus.

locus: A specific site on a chromosome.

lysing agent: A chemical used to open the cell membrane and cell nucleus and free the DNA.

manufactured DNA: Chemically manufactured DNA

using an instrument called a DNA synthesizer. Such DNA can be used as primers for PCR reactions or as probes in RFLP tests.

mapping of human genome: Effort to determine the function and location of all genes in human DNA.

marker DNA: A known size of DNA used as a control to determine the size of other fragments or bands of DNA. Also known as "sizing ladder."

membrane: See *nylon filter.*

mixed sample: A sample containing DNA from more than one person—such as mixed blood at a crime scene, or a vaginal swab taken from a rape victim.

molecular weight or MW: Molecular weight of a molecule; DNA, protein, DNA fragment.

molecular weight range: Range of molecular weights of DNA fragments at which a probe is effective.

molecule: A complex of atoms.

mutation: A change in the DNA sequence, also known as an allele.

nanogram: One billionth of a gram.

neurogenetics: Study of relationship between genetics and neurology.

nonpolymorphic probe: Also known as a monomorphic probe, its sequence is complementary to all human DNA and does not have alternative forms or alleles.

nucleotide: One of four bases—adenine, guanine, cytosine, or thymine—linked to sugar to which a phosphate group is added.

nucleus: The portion of the cell that contains the DNA.

nucleic acid synthesis: Method of making DNA—cloning chemically or by using PCR.

nylon filter: Nylon paper onto which the DNA is transferred during the Southern blotting procedure. Also known as a filter or membrane.

one tandem repeat or one repeat unit: A single sequence of base pairs that repeat themselves.

partial digestion: An undesirable result obtained when the restriction enzyme fails to cut the DNA completely.

PCR: Polymerase Chain Reaction; a method of making DNA using a process that mimics cellular replication.

phage lambda DNA: Viral DNA sometimes used for marker lanes.

phenotype: The expression of a gene.

Polymarker: Multiple loci examined in PCR. (Five loci are combined in a commercially available DNA typing kit.)

polymerase chain reaction: See PCR.

polymorphic probe: A known DNA sequence that recognizes a locus that is polymorphic.

polymorphism: A section of the DNA that varies greatly from person to person.

population genetics: The study of the frequency of genes and alleles in various populations.

pores in gel: Tiny comblike holes in an agarose gel designed to slow the movement of DNA fragments during electrophoresis.

probe: A specific sequence of DNA that attaches to unzipped DNA.

product rule: A liberal method of calculating population frequency of alleles across multiple loci that are not linked.

proficiency testing: Tests to aid in assuring competence of technicians performing experiments.

quality controls or quality assurance: Controls and checks that aid in assuring the reliability of the experimental process.

quantitatively confirm visual match: Confirming a visual match by computer analysis.

radioactive DNA: DNA, usually a probe in RFLP testing, that is tagged with radioactive phosphorous.

restriction enzyme: An enzyme that cuts DNA internally at a specific, known sequence site.

rehybridized membrane: A nylon membrane from which a DNA probe is removed (stripped) and hybridized to a second DNA probe.

RFLP: Restriction Fragment Length Polymorphism.

sequence of base pairs: The sequence of A, T, G, and C in the DNA molecule.

signal: Radioactive emission from a probe attached to DNA on a nylon membrane that causes X-ray film to darken. The darkened areas are called bands and correlate with the location of the probe on the original membrane.

sizing: Measuring size of band.

Southern blot: The process of transferring DNA fragments from agarose gel to a membrane or cellulose filter, leaving the fragments in the exact position they had in the gel.

subpopulation: A smaller segment of a related population (e.g., Hispanics from Spain versus Hispanics from Ecuador).

TAQ polymerase: A heat-stable enzyme used in PCR to copy one strand of DNA.

thermocycler: A machine that is programmed to heat and cool automatically. It is used to carry out the PCR steps.

thymine: One of the bases present in DNA; will only combine with adenine.

typing strip: A membrane containing immobilized DNA of known sequences.

visual match: Visual analysis of autorad to determine if DNA bands have comigrated in lanes.

VNTR: Variable Number of Tandem Repeats; genetically determined sequences of repetitive DNA.

washing membrane: A process in which excess DNA probe is removed from a membrane by washing using specific stringency requirements.

X and Y chromosomes: The chromosomes that determine the sex of an individual.

yield gel: An agarose gel used to determine the quantity and quality of DNA.

APPENDIX B

Questions and Answers About DNA

1. What is deoxyribonucleic acid (DNA)?

DNA is a molecule that carries a person's "genetic code." It is present in every cell of the body that contains a nucleus, which in humans includes all cells except red blood cells. The DNA in each of an individual's cells is identical regardless of whether the biological source is blood, hair, semen, or tissue. Every person's DNA is unique, except for that of identical twins.

The typical DNA molecule contains millions of nucleotides, the building blocks of the nucleic acid DNA. Each DNA molecule has two chains of nucleotides linked in a formation that twists and looks like a spiral staircase or ladder. The "rungs" of this spiral ladder are the critical components of the DNA molecule for the purposes of DNA profiling. Each rung is commonly referred to as a "base pair" or "base sequence," and the order in which the base pairs appear on the ladder constitutes the genetic code for the cell.

Each person's genetic code, also called the "genome," contains about 100,000 genes and approximately 3.3 billion base pairs. Most people are biologically very similar, and of all these base pairs, only about three million (or one percent) differ from one person to another; the differences are referred to as "polymorphisms." It is these polymorphisms that provide the basis for DNA identification and have great significance for DNA forensic analysis.

2. What biological material can be matched for DNA?

DNA is present in blood, semen, tissue, bone marrow, hair roots, saliva, urine, and tooth pulp.

3. What are the tests for DNA matching?

There are two tests used in DNA profiling. They are commonly referred to as "RFLP" and "PCR."

Restriction Fragment Length Polymorphism (RFLP) compares the sizes (total fragment length) of a polymorphism—the part of the DNA molecule that differs from person to person.

The RFLP test requires a larger DNA sample than the PCR test. For the RFLP test, approximately five thousand cells are needed. In addition, the sample must be fairly "fresh." That's because the RFLP tests longer fragments than the PCR test, and the longer the fragment the quicker the degrading of the matter. The test can take twelve or more weeks to complete.

In contrast to RFLP, the Polymerase Chain Reaction (PCR) test uses a much smaller sample of around fifty cells, and the cells tested need not be "fresh."

The PCR test identifies an actual gene where individuals tend to vary from each other, then replicates that gene thousands of times (which is why it is called a "chain reaction" test). Once replicated (or, as it is commonly referred to, "amplified"), the DNA is typed through genetic probes. If two samples have the same type, they may have come from the same source.

When first used, the PCR test was less precise than RFLP, because PCR tested only one gene, called the DQ-Alpha marker. Hence, the PCR test was, and still is, often used to exonerate rather than incriminate a suspect. That's because the threshold for excluding a suspect is much lower than that for including or incriminating an individual. With new developments, however, PCR testing is becoming more precise than it was a few years ago and more popular than RFLP. Today, six "markers," or genes, have been identified for PCR testing, and the test is now often referred to as the "PCR polymarker" test. Its popularity has increased for several reasons:

- It can be completed faster than RFLP (in two weeks versus two to three months).
- PCR polymarker requires a fraction of the sample that RFLP requires for testing (fifty cells versus five thousand cells).
- The PCR sample need not be as fresh as that used in RFLP.

4. Are DNA tests more reliable for exclusion than for inclusion of a suspect?

Yes and no. It is easier to see an exclusion and statistics are not involved. Also, if any DNA profile fails to match the defendant, he is excluded. For inclusion, all the DNA tests conducted must match the defendant. Some tests may be inconclusive in that the results can't be read, but the rest of the tests must match the defendant's profile. Further, statistical calculations are

necessary and that issue has not been firmly settled in the
courts. Hence, exclusions are easier to interpret, but they
are as reliable as inclusions, providing the tests are performed properly in both instances.

5. Have there ever been "false positives" through DNA matching?

In a 1987 study (at the very early stages of DNA
analysis, before integrity controls existed), there were
some false positives during blind testing of some laboratories. They were due to two errors: incorrect loading of
samples into testing machines and contamination of one
of the materials used in the test. There is no current evidence of false positives. The procedures used and
integrity controls employed are now considered extraor-
dinarily reliable. The error rates are well under one percent today, and that one percent figure accounts primarily
for false exclusions, not false inclusions. That is, a suspect is more likely to be falsely exonerated rather than
falsely accused. If the tests are performed correctly and
with integrity, there can never be a false-positive reading.
There has never been a case where properly performed
DNA tests inculpated an innocent person.

6. What is the meaning of contamination as it applies to DNA tests?

Contamination occurs when bacterial DNA somehow
finds its way into the sample. This can happen when the
evidence is retrieved from dirty streets or clothing, or
in the laboratory because of failure of quality control. It
can cause confusing results, as it usually creates extra
bands in the autorad that must be explained. If these extra
bands are not explained away by additional testing, the

tests may cause a false exclusion. A risk, although not a substantial one, also exists, that a false positive or inclusion may occur—although this has never been observed.

7. What is the controversy in the scientific community about DNA matching?

The battle is among population geneticists and forensic scientists. Population geneticists are concerned with allele frequency in a particular part of the population, such as African Americans, Caucasians, or Hispanics. The alleles they seem to concentrate on are the gene variations responsible for different traits such as hair, blood type, or eye color. Other scientists, including many forensic scientists, dispute this view and argue that the polymorphic sections of the DNA do vary substantially even among subpopulations of the same groups.

The essence of the debate surrounds the methods for estimating the population frequencies of specific DNA typing patterns.

Conservative population geneticists claim that the proponents of DNA matching erroneously presume that certain characteristics occur with regularity in a given ethnic group. Thus, the conservative group contends that the proponents' probabilities are much higher than is really the case and speculate that it will take ten to fifteen years and the study of about one hundred different ethnic groups to resolve the question and to assemble data on genetic variation among these ethnic groups to support claims of matching by chance. However, this dispute appears to be resolving itself as the FBI has completed a worldwide study of many ethnic groups and determined that there is great variation in the polymorphic sections of the DNA even within a specific ethnic group.

8. What is the relevance of statistical analysis?

It answers the question of the chances of anyone else having the same genetic pattern as the defendant. Hence an expert witness usually testifies that the chances of anyone having the defendant's DNA pattern is one in, say, 250 million or any other figure that is arrived at by multiplying various numbers obtained from each individual DNA test. Gigantic numbers can be produced, sometimes exceeding the number of people living on the earth. The higher the number, the more unique the DNA pattern. Some critics have said that statistics are unnecessary and confusing. They note that DNA forensic evidence is the only forensic science that imposes statistical estimates upon otherwise correct testing procedures.

9. What is the current state of the law regarding DNA admissibility?

No court has held that DNA testing is per se inadmissible. Those states that have refused to admit DNA evidence are concerned strictly with the statistical problems, and not the DNA test itself.

10. What is the importance of DNA testing beyond its forensic use?

The use of DNA in medicine is an exciting advance in the diagnosis and treatment of many previously incurable diseases. Many respected scientists consider DNA testing as the wave of the future.

11. Is DNA fingerprinting evidence as powerful as ordinary fingerprints?

Generally, fingerprint evidence is considered more powerful and reliable because no two people, including identical twins, have the same fingerprints, so it does not occasion statistical problems. However, it is clear that DNA evidence can be as powerful as fingerprinting evidence, especially when the statistical figures exceed the population of the earth. Indeed, in one case, the figures exceeded the amount of people that have ever lived on earth from the beginning of time. That's a powerful statement!

APPENDIX C

DNA Admissibility: Judicial Criteria

My suggested criteria for DNA admissibility, prepared for the *Castro* case, has become the model used in many courtrooms. Consider the impact these procedures might have made in the Simpson case had they been followed.

Partial text of opinion by Judge Gerald Sheindlin in *People of New York v. Joseph Castro*:

A pretrial hearing should be conducted to determine if the experiments and calculations performed by the testing laboratories in the particular case yielded results sufficiently reliable to be presented to the jury. The hearing will also serve to aid the trial judge in formulating appropriate instructions to the jury in the event sharp issues of fact emerge from the hearing.

Of course, the judge may also preclude the evidence, as a matter of law, if the evidence reveals that the testing laboratory failed to substantially comply with the scientifically accepted tests and procedures.

The following pretrial hearing procedures are suggested:

1. Notice of intent to offer DNA evidence should be served as soon as practicable.

2. The proponent, whether defense or prosecution, must give discovery to the adversary, which must include (1) copies of the autorads, with the opportunity to examine the originals; (2) copies of laboratory books; (3) copies of quality-control tests run on material utilized; (4) copies of reports by the testing laboratory issued to proponent; (5) a written report by the testing laboratory setting forth the method used to declare a match or nonmatch, with actual size measurements, and mean or average-size measurement, if applicable, together with standard deviation used; (6) a statement by the testing lab, setting forth the method used to calculate the allele pool for each locus examined; (7) a copy of the data pool for each locus examined; (8) a certification by the testing lab that the same rule used to declare a match was used to determine the allele frequency in the population; (9) a statement setting forth observed contaminants, the reasons therefore, and tests performed to determine the origin and the results thereof; (10) a statement setting forth any other observed defects or laboratory errors, the reasons therefore, and the results thereof; and (11) the chain of custody documents.

3. The proponent shall have the burden of going forward to establish that the tests and calculations were properly conducted. Once this burden is met, the ultimate burden of proof shifts to the adversary to prove, by a preponderance of the evidence, that the tests should be suppressed or modified.

It is noted that issues of fact which arise as a result of the hearing concerning the reliability of any particular test, or the size or ratio of the population frequency, relate to the weight of the evidence and not its admissibility. However, where the results are so unreliable, as was demonstrated in this case, the results are inadmissible as a matter of law.

APPENDIX D

DNA: The Law by Jurisdiction

No jurisdiction has ruled that DNA identification evidence is per se inadmissible.

The following jurisdictions, along with the United States Court of Appeals for the Second, Sixth, Eighth, and Ninth Circuits, have declared that DNA evidence is admissible both to include and to exclude identity:

Alabama	Massachusetts
Alaska	Michigan
Arizona	Minnesota
California	Missouri
Colorado	Montana
Florida	New Hampshire
Georgia	New Jersey (PCR)
Hawaii	New Mexico
Idaho	New York (RFLP and PCR)
Illinois	North Carolina
Indiana	Ohio
Iowa	Oregon
Kansas	Pennsylvania
Maryland	South Carolina

South Dakota	Washington
Texas (RFLP and PCR)	West Virginia
Virginia (RFLP and PCR)	Wyoming

The following jurisdictions have held that no pretrial hearing is required before the evidence is admitted:

Arizona (as to Cellmark)	New York
Colorado	Ohio
Iowa	South Carolina
Michigan	Texas
Missouri	West Virginia

The following jurisdictions have ruled that defects in the performance of the testing procedures go to the weight of the evidence and not to its admissibility:

Colorado	New York
Hawaii	Ohio
Illinois	Oregon
Indiana	Pennsylvania
Iowa	South Carolina
Minnesota	Washington
Missouri	West Virginia
New Hampshire	Wyoming

The following jurisdictions have ruled that DNA identification is reliable and should be admitted if the tests are performed properly, but will exclude the evidence if significant laboratory error is established:

Alabama	New Mexico (as to the FBI)
Minnesota	North Carolina

South Carolina   West Virginia
South Dakota

   The following jurisdictions have decided that DNA
evidence should be admitted but have placed limitations
on statistical evidence:

Arkansas   Nebraska
Arizona   New Hampshire
Delaware   Pennsylvania
District of Columbia

It strikes without warning.
A horrifying and lethal disease with no name and no cure.

EBOLA

A Documentary Novel of Its First Explosion

by William T. Close, M.D.

A terrifying and completely authentic novel of medical suspense by an American physician who lived in Zaire for sixteen years, and who worked desperately to contain the first outbreak of the Ebola virus in 1976.

At the Catholic mission in Yambuku, a remote area of Zaire, Mabalo Lokela, a local teacher, visits the clinic with a raging fever. Within days, Mabalo is dead. Soon after, others become ill and die. As panic erupts and the villagers try to flee, the roads leading out of Yambuku are blocked. Cut off from the outside world, the valiant nuns and medical personnel left behind at the mission can only pray and wonder. Will the world ever hear their plea for help?

The electrifying true account of how the
police investigate murder, by the first
reporter ever to gain unlimited access
to a homicide detective unit.

Basis for the award-winning TV series.

HOMICIDE
A Year on the Killing Streets

by David Simon
Edgar Award Winner

Baltimore: Twice every three days another citizen is shot, stabbed, or bludgeoned to death.
This is the true story of one year of murder in the
big city and the cops who hunt the killers.

Published by Ivy Books.
Available wherever books are sold.